52 SEED
THOUGHTS
for
Christian
Living

52 SEED THOUGHTS

for Christian Living

by R.E.O. WHITE

Wm. B. Eerdmans Publishing Co., Grand Rapids, Mich.

MOST of the following meditations and reflections first appeared in the pages of the Baptist Times, evoking a measure of appreciation which has led to this reproduction in permanent form. For the welcome given them, and for the permission of the Editor of that journal, Rev. W. W. Bottoms M.A., substantially to repeat them here, grateful acknowledgement is tendered.

Contents

1 The Dayspring

IT is an old man's name for Advent — "Dayspring" — and it seems to lend a lovely word an added beauty. Not often does age speak of new beginnings, but here is an old saint who for long years had waited for the promised consolation of his people. He had seen hope fade and the promise tarry. Now he feels a new expectancy quicken within him; he discerns in the birth of the Forerunner the imminent coming of the King. He sees the dawn glow in the eastern sky after a long night of dark and silent heavens, and hails with prophetic excitement a new Day breaking: "Through the tender mercy of our God, the dayspring from on high hath visited us, to give light to them that sit in darkness and in the shadow of death, and to guide our feet into the way of peace."

"A Star shall arise out of Jacob", declares the ancient seer at the beginning of the Book: "He is the Morning Star" replies the Christian seer at the end. The last pages of the Old Testament foresee that the Sun of righteousness shall arise, with healing in His beams; the first pages of the New announce, "He is the Sunrise, Springtime, Dayspring, Dawn of a new Day." And the glorious burden of the gospel is that *every* man's story can begin again — with Christ.

G. K. Chesterton beautifully describes the coming of St. Francis into the darkness and gloom of the Middle Ages. "It was the end of a long stern night. He stood with his hands uplifted; about him was a burst of birds singing, and behind him was the break of day." The miracle had been repeated: a morning light of promise began to dispel the shadows of medieval Europe, because another clear soul had seen, and steadily reflected, the radiance of the Dayspring from on high.

Thus had it seemed to the aged Zacharias. A lost and weary, darkened world stirred in its sleep, looked up, and saw far down the sky the flush of dawn, and in that morning saw the glory of the Lord — saw

> Above the edge of dark appear
> The lances of the sun . . . .
> There's something happy on the way,
> For God sends love to earth.

"To give light to them that sit in darkness . . .": unmoving because confused, halted because lost. To the night-bound traveller, the first streaks of dawn that lift up his heart pick out also the hedgerows and the landmarks that shall direct his way. The people that walked in darkness have seen a great light, for the Son of God has come and *has given us an understanding*. We have no business to be so perplexed in counsel, so darkened in judgement. Light has come, and they who follow were promised that they should no longer walk in darkness but have the light of life. The Babe has come to guide our feet into that path of light where none need stumble.

". . . And in the shadow of death . . . ." They *sit* because despairing, weighed down with grief. In her *Song of the Night at Daybreak* Alice Meynell asks where Night shall hide itself—

> *All my stars forsake me,*
> *And the dawn winds shake me,*
> *Where shall I betake me? . . .*

> *To a brow that is*
> *Bowed upon the knees*
> *Sick with memories.*

Yet even there Night will find no final refuge, if Christ the Dayspring speak His word of courage, faith, and coming good. The brow clears, the head is lifted, the future is bright; Day lies ahead, and we are children of the Day. Moreover the Day His coming ushers in is endless: "there is no night there". The Babe has come to guide our feet into a path that leads from an empty tomb on into the eternal morning, the shining path of an undying hope.

". . . Into the way of peace." Homing through the last hours of the night, a countryman saw ahead through the morning mists a dimly outlined figure that might at first have been a slowly moving beast. As the light strengthened he saw it to be a man, a stranger seemingly, perhaps unfriendly, possibly dangerous. But as the sun rose higher he recognised — his brother.

Just so: in the light of the Bethlehem idyl we recognise our kinship with the whole family of those who share His human nature. "Goodwill toward men" is the watchman's cry on Advent morning: and "peace on earth" becomes the marching order for the new Day. The Babe has come to herald a day of brotherhood and end the night of wrong, that men might walk in fearless, unsuspecting comradeship that path that leads to peace.

> The soft light from the stable door
> Lies on the midnight lands;
> The wise men's star burns evermore
> Over all desert sands.

Who hails with Zacharias the Dayspring from on high has set his face for ever toward the sunrising, and his feet on the path that shineth more and more unto the perfect Day.

2 Another Way

EVERYONE who visits Bethlehem must, surely, depart "another way". To return the way we came would mean our coming had made no difference: it would imply that His coming, too, had been in vain. For He came expressly to set our feet upon *new* paths, to start humanity upon a different road: to guide our feet into the way of peace, for one thing, and the way of salvation, the way to God, the way home. It would be shameful to come by any road to Bethlehem and go back the same old way — shameful and foolish, and these were wise, enlightened men.

They had come the way of wisdom, seeking the goal of all their learning, and they had found the Truth. They had come the way of history, to the city of David, and they had found Him in whom all history reveals its focus. They had come the way of the star, following what light they had, and they had found the Light of the world. They came the way of prophecy, and found the fulfilment of all past preparation; they came the way of worship, bearing costly gifts, and found God's unspeakable Gift to men. For all the highroads of the human spirit lead at last to Bethlehem — and back again.

So, "they departed to their own country another way". They returned along the road of faith *fulfilled*. In a sense they came in faith, as we do: a longing, wistful, seeking faith. But having seen the Christ-child once again we must go back with surer step and steadier tread. The promises have come to pass; deep intuitions of the spirit have been satisfied; God has landed on our shores, intervening in our sorely stricken world. History is not an endless chain close-binding us to things inevitable — God, we see, does new, surprising things. The world is not a closed circle shutting out its Maker — He is here! "We have seen the Lord; the Son of God is come, and hath given us an understanding; we know Him that is true." So faith holds up her head again, and marches back from Bethlehem to fight once more.

No less certainly did these wise men return along the way of hope *more surely founded*. They came with hope, enquiring whether it might be so: they departed with hope assured it is, and will be, so. For with God every fulfilment carries within it the promise of yet greater things. Every birth is both an end and a commencement; a baby, even a divine Baby, is only a beginning, after all. Ahead lay years of waiting for manhood and ministry, teaching and death, but all was implied and promised in His coming at all. Standing beside the manger they knew great things were afoot.

From the first centuries, Christian piety has seen in the gifts of the Magi the prophecy of what was yet to come: myrrh for His burying, incense for His priestly sacrifice and intercession, gold for His coming coronation. And from the beginning, too, of Christian liturgy the Church has kept the Advent season with two comings in her mind, one past and one to be. We return home from the stable not as those who have waited long and seen the end, but as those who have seen a great and promising beginning. So hope, too, lifts her head again, and dances back from Bethlehem to sing once more.

And of course the Magi returned the way of love *rekindled*. Something, surely, of goodwill and sacrifice was in their hearts as they sought Him out. They came not empty-handed. But they go back from Bethlehem with Love itself, not urged upon them as a duty but asserted, affirmed, revealed, declared, pledged in the infant Christ. The whole significance of His coming into a world with Herod and Caesar already in command was to show that God so loved *this* world. The Father sent the Son to be the Saviour of the world — herein is love. God wills our welfare: that is the one sure fact on which all faith can stand, and hope can rest, and in which love can find perpetual inspiration.

For we cannot linger indefinitely around the manger. He will not let us loiter there. He will Himself outgrow the cradle, and the stable, and soon be out among the poor, the hungry, the lepers and the lost. If we would stay beside Him, we, too, must leave the Christmas shrine and go back to where the work is waiting to be done. So love, again, lifts up her hands and swiftly runs from Bethlehem to do His bidding.

These are simple, but essential things. Without them Christmas is emptier than the rifled parcel, more tawdry than the wilting decorations. To come to Bethlehem, and then return along the same old roads, with no steadier faith, no brighter hope, no more tender, resolute love, would be to have come for nothing, and to go back unblessed.

3 A True Succession

THE Old Testament historians appear to have felt it necessary to apologise for Elisha, or at least to emphasise that he was truly a prophet. We are told that God instructed Elijah to anoint him. We are told how Elijah found him in the field and of his ready obedience to the call. We are reminded of the years of training as he "poured water on the hands of Elijah". We are given the simple, dramatic story of the refusal to leave Elijah at Gilgal, at Jericho or at Jordan until Elijah was taken up. Much is made of Elisha's possession of Elijah's mantle, and we are assured that in the end the sons of the prophets readily acknowledged that "the spirit of Elijah has fallen upon Elisha".

Was there then some doubt in Israel whether indeed Elisha was the true and fitting successor of the great champion of Jehovah?

If so, it was probably because of the very great differences between Elijah and Elisha. Elijah came, and spoke: and men recognised a prophet. He was above all else forceful, courageous; a lonely, stern man, dwelling in deserts or enduring years in silent solitude waiting his time. He was a great original, entirely independent alike of the schools of the prophets and of the favour of the people.

The things we remember about Elijah are his challenge to the nation at Carmel, and his challenge to King Ahab about Naboth's vineyard. If we remember, too, the sad scene upon Horeb, it is because of the strange alternation from fierceness, flint and fire to fearfulness, gloom and despair.

But Elisha is elaborately introduced and carefully supported. He dwells among men, in cities like Dothan and Samaria, a sociable man, and representative not of the older nomad wilderness life, but of the new, property-owning farming class. He could be stern, and he could wield political power; but his words are usually gentle and gracious, and the things we remember of him are miracles of healing and of kindness, having to do with homely things like porridge and loaves of bread, poverty, leprosy — and *forgiveness* of invading armies.

12

If Elijah was a religious politician, Elisha was a winsome pastor; if Elijah stormed, Elisha wooed and persuaded. And how the greybeards would shake their heads: prophets are not the men that once they were!

For at once the most obvious and the most distasteful lesson about all spiritual succession is that the new is never like the old. The first impression is one of contrast, followed soon by criticism. The upcoming seem never as good, as faithful, as powerful, as those who pass. Joshua succeeds Moses, but he is not Moses. Elisha succeeds Elijah, but he is not Elijah. Ezekiel succeeds Jeremiah, but he is certainly not another Jeremiah. The Church outlives the apostles, but apostles never appear again. That is how it must always be, and we do not like it.

Correspondents to religious periodicals earnestly discuss the dearth of great leaders at the present day, and whether the outstanding preachers of the past would now preach as once they did. Publishers reissue books of fifty years ago, recognising a steady popular demand that reflects the wistful wanting of what has passed forever. Church councils debate with wearisome repetition how the methods and organisations of forty years ago may be revived, although the one sure thing about them is that they produced the situation of today which we desire so desperately to change!

The simple, inescapable truth is that in God's work, as in all else, the new is never the same. We have to reckon on the fourth dimension, on time, and the change which time inevitably brings. True succession is never slavish imitation; and the inspiration of one generation is the bondage of the next. God's truth is a living word, and no dead shibboleth or unvarying formula. The Spirit bloweth where He listeth, not where He always did, and God is not bound to one generation, one fashion, or one method. There is shrewd wisdom in familiar words:

> The old order changeth, yielding place to new,
> And God fulfils Himself in many ways,
> Lest one good custom should corrupt the world.

For the stale good, too long persisted in when time demands fresh virtues, may shackle progress and serve to hide the weak evasion of new duties in a new age.

13

But we suspect divine novelties. We feel comfortable and secure among things we know. We are fearful of changes, more than a little scared of God's new morrow, more than a little distrustful of God's new men.

Yet though Elisha was not Elijah, the succession held. The truth and power and purpose of God were with the new no less than with the old. Beneath all that was changed of temperament and situation and method, certain things remained the same. Elisha wore the mantle of Elijah, remembered the vision of Elijah's ascension into heaven, sought and received a double portion of Elijah's spirit. Beneath the contrast and the criticism, perceptive eyes could see the continuity.

How often we cling to the mantle of the past without the vision! Or flourish the mantle, chatter about the vision, but remain empty of the spirit. It needs all three to constitute a true succession. Loyalty to our fathers does not require a constant harking backwards to their ways in a world that is no more; it means wearing their proud mantle, catching their high vision, emulating their true spirit, and so armed facing *today*, and then *tomorrow*, with confidence in their God.

We cannot make of the twentieth century a Galilean idyll, nor reduce the problems of our tortured world to the proportions of Bethlehem and Judea. But we can go forward unafraid, clothed in the mantle of our Master's likeness, carrying in our hearts the vision of His ascension to God's throne, seeking ever more earnestly a fuller portion of His Spirit. So doing, we can be assured that we are of the lineage of the prophets who were before us.

4 Men of Faith

OF all things one can imagine Jesus saying to our burdened and bewildered generation, the most probable seems to be the word spoken before the gates of Jerusalem to very surprised disciples. Their surprise arose from the discovery that a fig tree upon which He had pronounced "doom" had withered overnight. It was not the "why" that astonished them: they could well understand the power of acted parable and prophetic symbolism. They read His unspoken meaning, and knew what He foresaw for a religion and a nation that was luxuriant with ostentatious leaves of profession but barren of the fruit of godliness. They understood the "why" — it was the "how" that puzzled them. Even after so long with Jesus, they apparently did not expect His word to be so dramatically and effectually fulfilled. And answering their incredulous surprise Jesus says, "Have faith in God!"

For the heart of religious faith lies precisely in this daily expectation of "miracles", this reckoning upon divine fulfilment of the words of Jesus. Its nature might almost be defined as acceptance of the fact that God does act within this everyday, material world of ours. Faith is not feeling, nor fanaticism; it is not an influence, a technique, a habit of sanctimonious speech, or an escape from reality. It is reckoning upon God, in every perplexity counting upon divine direction, in every emergency relying on divine help, in every necessity seeking divine resources, in every extremity being conscious of God's presence. Faith *is* reckoning on God.

The only way to learn such faith, its meaning and its secret is to study the men of faith themselves. Fortunately a whole gallery of such men — and women — is exhibited before us, a cloud of witnesses to the life of faith, in Hebrews 11: and in them we can see faith at work.

One characteristic of these heroes arrests immediate attention: the men of great faith are most often men who have little or no faith in themselves. Moses at the bush protests, "Who am I, that I should go unto Pharaoh?. . . They will not believe me . . . . I am not eloquent . . .". Gideon likewise: "O Lord, wherewith shall I save Israel? Behold, my family is poor in Manasseh, and I am the least in my father's house . . . ." So was it, too, with Jeremiah, who felt himself a child, afraid of men's faces. Isaiah at his call cried, "Woe is me . . .". Paul knew himself less than the least of all the saints. When Jesus found a man who could say sincerely, "Lord, I am not worthy . . .", He

15

replied, "I have not found so great faith, no not in Israel".

Perhaps our major difficulty arises here. Great faith seems to grow beside great self-mistrust, and we moderns are so confident that the answer to all problems lies within ourselves — if only we could find it. Or sometimes, at the other extreme, we are so despondent of ourselves we cannot see beyond ourselves to God. "Have faith," says Jesus, *"in God"*.

It probably follows from their small faith in themselves that the men of great faith seem so often to have won their faith through conflict. Hebrews 11 is no roll-call of saints whose lives were unbroken sunshine and smooth water. They were strangers and pilgrims, suffered affliction, quenched the violence of fire, were tortured, stoned, sawn asunder, were destitute. Elijah is the New Testament's example of faith at prayer, yet he had his occasional juniper tree. Jeremiah camped under his. Paul speaks of fightings and fears, cares and being cast down.

Faith is not high spirits, though the two are frequently confused. Faith is so much more a matter of character than of intellect; a thing of courage, tenacity, loyalty to principle, not always of inspiration or high feeling-tone. The man who, with something near despair within his heart, goes on doing what God would have him do, still obeying when every light of consolation is withdrawn, is the man of faith in the end. His ultimate confidence and final peace are the long awaited fruit of great conflict. Great faith in God is never easy; its difficulty gives it depth.

A third reflection suggested by the Hebrews review of great examples is that the men of great faith have always been prodigious workers. These men are the outstanding figures of Israel's history. One thinks of the vast responsibilities of Moses, the heroic achievements of Samuel, the toil of Nehemiah, the stripes, imprisonments, shipwreck, labours, journeyings, vigils, preaching, writing, organising and praying of the apostle Paul. Place alongside these William Carey's colossal "plodding", and John Wesley's immeasurable journeyings, endless preaching, and immense toil — and you begin to glimpse the accuracy of Paul's phrase: "Faith worketh . . . ."

16

Faith's hands are always busy, never folded in the calm assurance that God will do whatever need be done. It is idleness, nine times out of ten, that breeds modern unbelief. "Intellectual difficulties" are but rationalisations, oftentimes, of simple spiritual sloth. "Faith worketh . . . ."

One further characteristic of the great believers is especially striking: they are all men with abounding confidence in the future. Joseph "gave commandment concerning his bones", and their ultimate disposal in the land of promise, at a time when it seemed impossible that Israel would ever see Canaan again. Jeremiah bought the field in Anathoth while yet the enemy's soldiers strutted its borders, the city was beseiged, and the prophet himself in prison. Abraham, "being called of God to seek a country which he should *after* receive for an inheritance, went out . . .". All confessed they were strangers and pilgrims in the earth, looking for a city.

For faith builds tomorrow, not on the fears of today but on the experience of yesterday. To believe in God is to believe in the future — for our trust is in the everlasting God, and He will be our guide, even unto death. Have faith in God!

5 Spiritual Scenery

THE Jew was never a sailor, and to the Hebrew mind the sea was always mysterious, disquieting, never friendly but constantly to be feared. Its unfathomable depths, peopled with monstrous creatures; its unresting changefulness; its wild, rebellious moods; its threat of danger and destruction; the mystery of what lay beyond its limitless horizon; perhaps a racial memory of the coming of the fierce Philistines invading across its waters; man's helpless inability to set bounds to its raging power — all this impressed the Hebrew poets, and lends meaning to the promise that in the perfect world "there shall be no more sea". So when the Psalmist says, "God's judgements are a great deep", awe and fear and helplessness are in his words.

He is confessing his ignorance of God's unfathomable ways. He cannot plumb God's thoughts, nor explain how God has dealt in suffering and sorrow and disillusionment with his own soul. He is confessing his helplessness, for as none can say to the sea, "Keep back", or to the waves, "No further", so none can say to the Almighty, "Thou shalt not". And in the word "judgements" is a hint of fear. God's ways with the wicked and the sternness of His law recall the awesomeness of mighty waters: man can but stand upon the shore of time and marvel at the irresistible tides in the affairs of men, the invisible currents that bear God's purposes onward without effort. "O the depth of the riches and wisdom and knowledge of God! How unsearchable are his judgments and how inscrutable his ways!"

Yet the Psalm is no dirge, no petulant complaint about the mysterious ways of God. The poet will not sit moaning beside the turbulent sea of life's strangeness, sorrow, and regret and weep that all is lost. He turns his gaze elsewhere. *The scenery of life is not all sea*; and when the rest of the landscape is painted in, the picture finds balance, and calmness, and beauty.

"Thy righteousness is like the great mountains" — a mountain range of certainty beside the restless sea. One unshakeable, immoveable, immeasurable thing balances in experience the other fluid, changeful, unfathomable thing. Life can be wild and mysterious and frightening as the sea, but God is ever right and true and just, His law as steadfast as the hills.

Most of us find that out the hard way. We try to get around, or past, or over the righteousness of God; we pretend we can get away with things. God pulls us up short, and we pay for our folly. God is not mocked, and His righteousness is a saving discipline.

But the great men of history have ever felt this righteousness at the heart of things as a surrounding, undergirding strength. Lincoln deeply regretted the prolongation of the Civil War, but he said: "If God wills it that war continue until all the wealth piled up by the bondman's two hundred and fifty years of unrewarded toil shall be sunk, and until every drop of blood drawn with the lash shall be paid by another drawn with the sword, then as it was said three thousand years ago so must it still be said, that the judgements of the Lord are true and righteous altogether."

Place beside that Churchill's "All comes out even at the end of the day, and all will come out yet more even when all the days are ended". The divine righteousness is a steadying, soaring mountain to set beside the sea of God's mysterious judgements.

"Thy faithfulness reacheth unto the clouds" — flying above the tossing sea, skimming the tops of the mountains — is the changeless loyalty of God to His own. He altereth not. He remaineth. He fainteth not, neither is weary. He will not fail thee, nor forsake. Before His face the generations rise and pass away, but none have found Him faithless, fickle, or untrue.

"God is faithful", declares Paul to the unstable Corinthians. "He is faithful who called you" is the message sent to the over-excited Thessalonians. "Though we are faithless, yet he abideth faithful," Paul reminds the nervous Timothy, adding, "He cannot deny himself". "He is faithful that promised" is the word for the doubting Hebrew Christians; "He is faithful to forgive" is the assurance of the apostle John.

If God visits the iniquity of the fathers upon the children unto the third and fourth generation, none the less surely does He show mercy unto thousands of them that love Him, and to children's children. For He has pledged Himself to show forth His faithfulness to all generations. So if sometimes across sea and mountains there pass the shadows of adversity, yet are they shadows cast by the faithfulness of God — faithfulness piled high as the clouds, as His judgments are deep as the sea.

"Thy mercy, O Lord, is in the heavens." High over sea and mountain and cloud stretches the impenetrable blue of Mediterranean skies, by day glowing with silver, by night studded with stars. Here is yet another immeasurable certainty to set beside the frightening sea: the everlasting mercy. Put that, too, into the picture of life, above the tossing waves!

In an unforgettable passage John Buchan describes the inmost thought of Edward Leithen, given a year to live and heading far north to offer it freely and joyfully in one last effort of man-hood. "There suddenly broke in on him like a sunrise a sense of God's mercy — Out of the cruel North most of the birds had flown south from ancient instinct, and would return to keep the wheel of life moving. Merciful! But some remained, snatching safety by cunning ways from the winter of death. Merciful! Under the fetters of ice and snow there were little animals lying snug in holes, and fish under the frozen streams, and bears asleep in their lie-ups, and moose stamping out their yards, and caribou rooting for their grey moss. Merciful! And human beings, men women and children, fending off winter and sustaining life by an instinct old as that of the migrating birds. One man nursing like a child another whom he had known less than a week . . . . Surely, surely, behind the reign of law and the coercion of power there was a deep purpose — of *mercy*."

What is this but a modern expression of what another Psalmist felt: "The Lord is plenteous in mercy . . . . As the heaven is high above the earth . . . as far as the east is from the west . . . from everlasting to everlasting . . . ." Fathomless, boundless, limitless, timeless is the mercy that encompasses all experience, that does not deal with us as our sins deserve, nor reward us according to our iniquities. From the horizon behind us to that in front, and on every side, life's over-arching sky is the lovingkindness of our God — the ultimate fact in all God's dealings with men.

Surely, with the mountains of His righteousness, and the high clouds of His faithfulness, and the over-arching sky of His mercy in the picture of life, we can trust Him with the mysterious sea!

6 Go Deeper

LET us go on", says the writer to the Hebrews, "unto matu-rity", rebuking at once the unusableness and the instability of shallow Christian experience. So Paul wrote to Corinth of the quarrelsomeness of spiritual babes which was turning that Church of Christ into an ill-disciplined nursery. So, again, he pleaded that the Ephesians might grow up to the stature of Christ, not blown about by every wind. On to maturity means deeper into truth, into faith, into experience with God: and concerning that need the Church has ever had before it the unforgettable word of Jesus about seed that springs immediately to luscious greenness, only to fade for want of depth.

"Go deeper!" Three Congo missionaries from widely different districts report to the home base of this common need. Sometimes, they say, evangelism can "roll along on its own"; but teaching and training must follow the good news, lest converts are lost and church life wither. From the frontiers of the kingdom, where Christian loyalties confront the age-old paganism, the call for maturity gains pathos and urgency — and a touch of fear.

"Go deeper!" A trusted leader of an African mission, rejoicing in the number of missionary recruits, yet adds with wistful honesty: "Our real trouble is that the student missionaries, with three years in Bible school or college and the long experience of the home churches behind them, are less mature than many of our native Christians — less wise in the scriptures, less experienced with God, less able to meet the challenge of the enemy." From the front-line of leadership in the younger churches the call to maturity is sharpened with rebuke, and a touch of disappointment.

"Go deeper!" Two wise and well-informed scholars agree that a world-faith is essential, and it must be Christian. But, they add, "Christianity as it stands is not fit for that function. The sober truth is that a great deal of Christianity . . . is as unfitted to guide the future of religion in the world as the Marxists of Russia and their friends are to dispose of it". From the intellectual uplands where human ideologies resist the revelation of God in Christ, the demand for maturity of thought and faith gains intense seriousness, and a touch of warning.

But what is this maturity and depth to which the time, the teachers, and the hunger of our hearts alike invite us?

Certainly it implies a Christian life and thought as deep as the scriptures — and that is a great deal deeper than a beaker of gospel texts and a few Bible illustrations of salvation. There are heights and depths in the Bible, high as the purpose of God and deep as the deceitfulness of sin, which demand diligence of study and thoroughness of understanding. But it is to be feared that great tracts of scripture, where honest men wrestle with huge problems and hammer out answers to soul-shaking questions, are almost forbidden reading to our so easily troubled hearts.

As certainly, depth of spiritual life implies a faith as deep as human experience, that does not vanish at the touch of adversity, nor faint at the contradiction of childish hopes, nor wither away because prayer remains unanswered. Only a shallow gospel pretends that all goes well for those who come to Jesus, nourishing the soul on fictional fodder only one degree above the popular romance of happy endings. The rain descends, the winds blow, the floods rise around the wise man's house: the spiritual weather is just the same for the evil and the good. But where faith is as deep as the pain, the sin, the sorrow of life, the house of the soul will stand.

A deeper message will come to terms with the issues that beset society, issues we are so adroit in evading, so careful not to see: the perils of atomic science, the exploitation of sex for gain, the vitiation of freedom for the sake of license, the decay of authority and of discipline among adults and youth alike, the lack of social purpose and hope, the appalling want of moral indignation, insight, and integrity. In a world of spiritual peril and insidious temptation, an ABC gospel plus a hundred appeals to be clean and Christlike are not enough. We must go deeper, in instruction, in training, in devotion and in discipline — if only for safety's sake.

And depth implies the personal knowledge of the "deep things of God", the kind of spiritual shrewdness and simplicity that understands God's character and ways, and sees His hand in the phases of experience. Such insight is only to be gained by long, long thoughts about history and duty and one's own spiritual pilgrimage; by clear self-knowledge and humility; by walking close with God, often in shadowed places. Here, most of all, we modern Christians must go deeper, as deep as the heart of God: lest we fail our generation, disappoint ourselves, and betray our Lord.

7 He Shall Stand

PAUL'S afterthoughts always arrest attention. He is so fluent a writer, so swift a debater, that often he leaves us toiling behind; but now and again there is a pause, a sentence of correction, an illuminating aside, a thought in parentheses, an unexpected turn of phrase. And what light such involuntary comments throw upon a passage — and on Paul! One such occurs in Romans 14:4: "God shall make him stand."

The argument concerns the relations of Christians to each other, especially about those things in which brethren disagree. There are differences of belief, about which all tend to be dogmatic — beliefs about meat slaughtered at idol-temples, for example: important enough in practice, but scarcely to be exalted into cause of strife among Christians. There are differences about conduct, in which all tend to become self-righteous; and here the examples are eating, drinking, Sabbath-observance. And there are differences of conscience, about which all tend to be superior. Conscience is so personal, so emotional, and the confidence that we are taking our stand on conscientious grounds is so pleasant (even when completely mistaken!) that few things divide Christians more effectively than conscientious scruples.

There is plenty of room here for contention, and Paul contends manfully. No less than six enlightening principles are laid down. Every man must be fully persuaded for himself, and if in doubt, leave well alone. Each must be jealous for his brother's welfare, lest by example he lead any astray. Nothing is unclean of itself, but in the attitude of mind that it evokes; peace and mutual encouragement must limit Christian freedom, and none must judge his brother. On all such points of faith and conduct a man shall answer to his own Lord; we observe the holy day, we eat, or we abstain, we live or die, each to our Lord. Let none judge another's servant, for we shall every one give account of himself before the judgement seat of Christ. To his own master each standeth, or falleth . . . .

Then, suddenly, the afterthought: "Yea, God shall make him stand." Generous, magnanimous, full of pastoral compassion, the challenging phrase lifts the whole discussion to new levels and a better spirit. True, to his own master he standeth or falleth, *but he shall not fall*: he shall be holden up! Whatever you think of him, of his opinions, or foibles, or vagaries of conscience; whether he is in the majority or the few, narrow or broad, over-scrupulous or easy-going; whether he agrees with you or not, God shall make him stand!

Doughty controversialist, intrepid defender of real principles, though he was, Paul is away ahead of most of us in this tolerant, large-hearted comment. It means, for one thing, that in all such discussions of belief, conduct, conscientious scruples, we all need to preserve, against our inclinations, the constant underlying awareness that the other fellow may after all be right. "I pray you, gentlemen, in God's name, conceive the possibility that you may be wrong." Nothing needs saying in religious controversy more often than that; but few things are said less often, or are harder to accept. Yet we find, at the end of the day, that truth frequently is on the other side! The argument goes against us, not as we suppose because all others are stupid, weak, unspiritual, faithless, but because they were right.

But Paul means more. He implies that God will make the brother stand even if in this particular matter of dispute his opinions and scruples are misled, because God is on his side. God cares for him; Christ died for him; the divine love will not let him down simply because he is mistaken, or to vindicate you, or "to show where right lies". God loves him if you do not. Though you might delight to thrust him down, God shall make him stand.

There lies exposed the deepest principle of all. Every disputatious issue that divides brethren, be it eating, drinking, custom, doctrine, observance, or scruple, every such matter of contention is utterly secondary and subordinate to a right attitude toward each other. The kingdom of God is not meat and drink, but righteousness, peace, and joy in the Holy Ghost. However cogent your arguments, however deep your convictions, however tender your conscience, however irreproachable your conduct, if you walk uncharitably, all profits you nothing. Meticulous rightness about details is more than cancelled out by omission of the weightier matters of mercy, compassion and concern. "Whosoever doeth not righteousness is not of God; neither he that loveth not his brother." Whatever you may think of him, God shall make him stand.

8 This Same Jesus

OUR Lord's entry into Jerusalem represented, among other things, a great renunciation. Both His followers and His enemies expected some show of force, a dropping of the peasant's cloak and an assumption of Messianic majesty. But that way to a throne had been rejected, privately, long before in the wilderness temptation. Now it is rejected publicly, at the risk of losing many misunderstanding friends.

Thus behind the immediate significance of the dramatic scene there lies a permanent meaning, an abiding challenge. The ride upon the docile donkey, with palms about His head, the garments of pilgrims before His feet, the singing of the children in His ears, expresses something very near indeed to the innermost truth of Christian faith, enshrines Christ's very spirit, sounds one vital note in His message for mankind.

Here is majesty, power, strength, authority, clothed with the forms of gentleness, humility, servitude, peace. Here is the lowliness of true greatness. Here is the hiding of supreme power.

Much that the most ardent nationalist longed to see was here spread before his eyes. A mounted Messiah rides to the seat of David while an excited populace spread their clothes before Him as their fathers had done before Jehu on the way to his coronation, and wave their palms about Him as an earlier generation had waved them above the Hammerer of the Syrians, Judas Maccabaeus. Ancient prophecy is being fulfilled; the ancient welcome to Judah's kings is heard again before the city walls. Yet there is something wrong. The war horse is a donkey, the escort but a dozen Galilean peasants, the King Himself no warlike figure of inspiring majesty but a prophet-carpenter-teacher from an obscure home in some forgotten village. Somehow, the substance is there, without the form. It is, and it is not, a Royal Progress. For those with eyes to see, the daring claim is clear; but all is done in lowliness, without pomp, without threats. Friend and foe alike are baffled at His meaning.

Yet so He ever was. Had He not once remarked that among the Gentiles the exercise of lordship and the demand for dominion was the accepted mark of "benefactors", as rulers, with unconscious irony, loved to be called — and added sharply: "it shall not be so among you: but he that is greatest among you shall be your servant; the least and lowest shall be your chief"?

All *true* greatness has this quality. Intellectual superiority? — "Be not ye called Rabbi, Rabbi"; social position? — "Go, sit in the lowest seat . . . many that are first shall be last"; religious pride? — "Even the Son of man came not to be ministered unto, but to minister." Before that week was through, He would rebuke all wrangling about pre-eminence in His kingdom by laying aside His garments, taking a towel, and washing their feet. It is hard indeed to emulate *that* quality of greatness.

And so He is. This matchless Christ remains the same, the strong yet gentle, glorious yet lowly King of men. Where He holds sway in loyal hearts, we, too, ride on donkeys with the common folk as friends.

It does not always seem so. We become pushful and proud, "sensitive" to injury, aggressive, fond of style and circumstance. But the Master is still the Christ upon the ass: He has not changed — only now there are scars and nailprints to show how

26

far His willingness to serve will go. If we crown Him King of our lives and Lord of our hearts, this is the Christ we crown — the only Christ there is.

And so He ever will be. When He rides at last to the universal throne — as ride He will — He yet will come riding upon an ass, with the lowliness of divine greatness still upon His spirit. Some look even yet for the Warrior-Messiah for whom the Jews so ignorantly waited, the Christ who shall blast the wicked with the word of His mouth, and burn up the chaff with unquenchable fire. They have not understood Jesus very well, nor caught His spirit, nor entered into His great faith.

But then, not many have. We still trust in outward majesty and the trappings of power, in noise and pomp and mass-psychology, in blaring publicity, in drums and the mailed fist and the loudest shout and the biggest bombs. So rarely do we believe in the victory of lowliness: that gentleness is strength, that humility is dignity, that service is honor, that integrity is power, that truth is prevailing, innocence invincible, love almighty.

We forget that Jesus on His donkey trampled the proud legions of the mighty Caesars and rode peaceably to a throne in the hearts of all generations. That is why it is good for us to take our places again in the pilgrim procession and walk humbly behind the donkey with hosannas in our hearts.

9 Forsaking

WHEN the disciples "forsook all and followed him", the break was for most of them complete, and costly. For some it meant a break with home, and loyalty to Christ may still occasionally impose that painful duty. For others, as Levi and John, it involved a break with their work and security, as in certain situations faithfulness to Jesus may even yet require. For all *it* meant forsaking the free, uninhibited, irreligious way of life to accept a yoke, a discipline, and a task: for some hearts that is still the most forbidding implication of discipleship.

But these forsook all. We admire the instancy of their obedience. We warm to the ardour of their response. We wonder at the commanding strength of Jesus that could win such devotion from such men. Here we face clearly the absoluteness of the religious claim; here is the kindling dream, a fresh and convincing voice, a glowing hope. We envy the impulse and expectation that filled their hearts as they forsook all and followed.

Turn a few pages, and read again. "They all forsook him, and fled." It is in the garden, and the shadows beneath the trees are no darker than the shadows that have gathered around the Lord. He stands in danger, and His heart is heavy with sorrow. These same men see Him taken; they try to interfere and are checked; they break and flee. We must not condemn their flight, for He Himself released them. Their desertion was short-lived; they could do nothing for Him; and anyhow we would certainly have done the same.

Nevertheless, the record remains: "They forsook all . . . . They all forsook him." How comes it that those who begin so ardently can fail so meanly?

Time is one explanation. Two or three years had passed, and in two or three years very much can happen within the soul. Time tests the quality of metal, the resistance of stone, the endurance of heroes, and the sincerity of saints. Much that we thought was spiritual ardour turns out to have been just youthful spirits; much that we thought was absolute surrender proves to have been emotional impulsiveness. It takes time to make Christians; and sometimes time unmakes them. "He that endureth to the end shall be saved" is a footnote that should be added to every glowing testimony: "ye have need of patience".

For time brings *disappointments* that test faith's loyalty. These men had followed, in part, a golden dream: it led to a garden of gathering darkness. Just when they confessed He was the Christ He began to prophesy a cross. When the crowd would take Him by force to make Him king, His answer was to

28

disappear into the mountains, and next day to talk about His body given to nourish the world!

Many that day forsook Him, being disappointed. And it is to be feared that others share their feeling. The form of our evangelism is largely to blame: we offer what we cannot guarantee — ceaseless joy, exhilaration and abounding, unbroken, blessed assurance; a lifelong success in every high endeavour and victory without struggle. And some who set out with eager hearts are left unready for the facts that the way is uphill and the standards high. In the reaction of dismay, they forsake and flee. Anne Brontë is as honest as her Lord:

> Believe not those who say
> The upward path is smooth,
> Lest thou should'st stumble in the way
> And faint before the truth.
> It is the only road
> Unto the realms of joy;
> But he who seeks that blest abode
> Must all his powers employ.

Behind the disappointments lay *confusion*, and shallow thinking. It is truly surprising how often in those last days with Jesus the disciples are found misunderstanding His words, or not comprehending at all His teaching. "We cannot tell what he saith . . . Lord, how is it? . . . We know not . . . and how can we know? . . . Have I been so long time with you, and yet hast thou not known me? . . . I have many things to say, but ye cannot bear them now." Such is the tenor of their final conversations, and it explains much of the weakness and unwariness of the disciples' behaviour.

Uninstructed minds make for weak and vacillating hearts. *Because* they were slow to grasp His meaning, and His promise, they fled from His side in the hour of crisis. Yet He had warned repeatedly that the crisis would come, not only upon Peter, whom Satan would sift as wheat, but upon them all. Without exception they must sit down and count the cost, must remember that to look back is to be unworthy, and bring with them their cross if they would follow Him. He could not have taught more plainly, or more candidly, the cost of discipleship and the dangers of loyalty: but they were slow of heart to believe.

29

Realism is the seed of heroism, and Jesus hides nothing of the perils of the way. But if His word abide in us, we shall abide in Him, and He will see us safely through.

"They *all* forsook. . . ." Fear and disloyalty spread an epidemic cowardice: time, disappointment and confusion are reinforced by the *contagion* of moral weakness. Because we have so often (and so rightly) urged the corporate strength of Christian life, the thrill of the crowded gathering, where the individual is shielded from himself and sometimes from his Lord; because we have played up for all it is worth the contagious nature of religion, we have sometimes left young hearts too vulnerable to another powerful group-influence, that of unbelief. They may become incapable of a lonely, individual loyalty, prey to a secret, awful dread of standing *alone* beside the Christ when the world's soldiers bind Him and take Him away. Wonderful, and even necessary, as Christian fellowship is, too great dependence on the support of others is itself a serious weakness and can leave the soul in peril when loneliness and isolation give evil its opportunity.

In the season of the Passion we may well ask ourselves which phrase describes our present mood: are we still ready to forsake all at His command? or are we readier now, with the passing of difficult years, to forsake Him? Before we answer, it is good to set beside these phrases His own use of the same expression, as though in preparation for their testing and its consequent regret: "I will not forsake you, comfortless: I will come to you." He abideth faithful, and by His grace we, too, may continue steadfast to the end.

10 Why This Waste?

IT was an insensitive, uncomprehending question with which to challenge Mary: "Why this waste?" Yet in our more niggardly, utilitarian moods, when lavish expenditure on some religious edifice or event has contrasted sharply with the beggarly resources of some good cause for which we covet support, we have all sympathised with Judas, and earned the rebuke of Jesus. It will be a sorry day for every worthwhile social project when impulsive, even prodigal, devotion to Christ no longer moves the human heart or feeds the springs of Christian charity.

The suggestion that this act of love towards Jesus was at the expense of "the poor" was particularly inept. Never had "good news to the poor" been preached with more gracious accents or proved in more loving deeds than by the Friend of all the underprivileged of the earth. The heart that now was pouring its fragrant offering over His feet would very soon learn — if it did not know already — that to give food to the hungry, drink to the thirsty, shelter to the stranger, clothes to the naked, to visit the sick and the imprisoned, was the kind of devotion He would accept as "unto me". Perhaps Matthew's silent comment is sufficient: he sets the criticism of Mary, with its pretended concern for the needy, beside the sordid bargain that won the critic thirty pieces of silver, as if to let us judge for ourselves which of these two served the poor with greater zeal — she who anointed the feet weary in their service, or he who sold their Champion to His enemies.

"Why this waste?" — there can after all be no real answer. All lovely things are justified simply by their loveliness. The generous deed, spontaneous, warm-hearted, far-seeing, has no *reason*: or perhaps we should say the heart has its own reasons. In Mary's action love argued its own case, and to the mind of Jesus no material consideration could outweigh the personal devotion that gave the deed significance. And what made that devotion memorable "wheresoever this gospel shall be preached" was this: that of all the circle moving around Jesus in those last fateful days, Mary alone had the sympathy to read His burdened heart, the wit to discern the sorrow just ahead, and the love, inarticulate and yet eloquent, to show she understood. "Against the day of my burying hath she kept this." In the loneliness of His passion He had found one kindred spirit, and He rewarded her tender insight with immemorial praise.

Mary knew He was to die and perceived with a woman's swift appreciation of true values the extravagance of the gift He was making to the world. If we venture to raise Judas' question to the cross itself, and ask not concerning the ointment and the cruse but concerning the breaking of the Lord's body and the spilling of the fragrance of that divine life, "To what purpose was *this* waste?" — we shall receive the reply: God's heart, too, has its reasons; and divine love no less than human delights to overflow in loving deeds.

The New Testament writers are plainly impressed by this extravagant aspect of the cross. One after another they reveal their awareness that Calvary involved a prodigal expenditure of the most priceless treasure in earth or heaven. And one after another they attempt to define the purpose of this "waste".

John declares that God *so* loved the world that He gave His *only-begotten* Son; and immediately he links so great love and so immense a gift with the universal scope of God's salvation — "whosoever believeth" — and with the inexhaustible blessing it conveys — "everlasting life". The measureless end explains the lavish means.

Paul daringly hints at divine consideration of the price involved, and roundly affirms that God "spared not" His own Son, but "delivered him up" for us all, an "unspeakable gift". And at once he draws the bold conclusion: "how shall he not with him also freely give us all things!" So limitless a sacrifice implies unstinting care.

The writer to the Hebrews, again, deliberately compares all earlier priesthood with that of our High Priest — "holy, harmless, undefiled, separate from sinners, higher than the heavens" — and the ancient repetitive sacrifices with the one eternal sacrifice of Christ, never to be repeated, supplemented, or excelled. "Such a high priest befitted us," he argues, "able to save to the uttermost all who come unto God by him, seeing he ever liveth to make intercession for them." The magnitude of the salvation attained requires such dignity in the Saviour.

And Peter expressly emphasises that we were redeemed "not with corruptible things as silver and gold" — making the commercial, utilitarian comparison explicit — "but with the precious blood of Christ." And he, too, finds significance in this lavish payment made for man's redemption: for as his constant use of the word "incorruptible" makes clear, Peter is impressed with the unfading *permanence* of the Christian's wealth in Christ. He is born of an incorruptible seed, adorned with an incorruptible beauty of spirit, waits for an incorruptible inheritance: for he is redeemed especially from the *vanity* of mere tradition and the futility of merely earthly hopes. Only an immeasurable ransom could purchase such unfading bliss.

The divine extravagance, then, like Mary's, involves no waste. It is but the love that sets no limits, the determination to serve that hesitates at no cost. In response to all Christ gave, to all God did, what cruse of ours can be too costly to be broken, what ointment too precious to be outpoured in loving service at His feet? We lose what on ourselves we spend: this, and this alone, is wanton waste.

11 World Crucified

THAT the Christian is crucified with Christ, no one who understands his baptism may ever forget. But when Paul adds to this thought, *"the world is crucified to me"*, his phrase arrests attention. It might be taken to imply a narrow and self-centred isolation from all things human, the denial of all responsibilities, delights and duties in society. But Paul knew that if our citizenship be in heaven, our service is here on earth to shine as lights, to walk circumspectly toward them that are without, to redeem the age and serve in all good conscience the generation to which we belong.

The clue to Paul's meaning lies rather in the situation of the apostolic Church. A small, new society, embracing few who were wise or noble or placed in power, it struggled for its life in a hostile world. Christians were outnumbered, outweighed, outcast, in an environment actively contemptuous and full of menace. They did not marvel if the world hated them: they were used to it!

They might so easily have retaliated with threats of doom and self-righteous scorn. Perhaps occasionally they did. But New Testament Christians knew that God loved the world, and sent His Son not to condemn but to save it. Somehow they found a secret of loving it — and not loving it; of living in it while separated from it; of standing up to it unafraid and free, superior and yet compassionate. Part of that secret was that in their eyes the world had crucified itself.

For example: Paul was very conscious of being identified with a despised minority, the "filth and offscouring of the world". Jewish pride of religion and Greek intellectual conceit both touched him where it hurt. But what, he asks, is this boasted wisdom of the world — religious or philosophic? Did it not take the Christ of God and nail Him to a tree? Was *that* clever, or far-seeing, or prudent? The world's wisdom over-reached itself at Calvary, and stands exposed as foolishness. Had the rulers of this world known true wisdom, they would have had more sense!

So Paul admitted to no intellectual inferiority: "We speak wisdom among them that can understand it." What does it matter if the world know us not, when it did not recognise Him? Man's wisdom crucified itself in the supreme folly of the cross, and henceforth before the intellectual snobbery of unbelief we need not feel ashamed. Whatever our mental shortcomings, we have seen the truth in Christ, and glimpsed the wisdom that is God's.

Nor are we, Paul argues, in bondage to the world's power. There are many adversaries, but we are led in triumph in Christ. "Behold I go bound in the spirit . . . not knowing what shall befall me, save . . . bonds and afflictions. But none of these things move me, neither count I my life dear unto myself . . . . I am ready not to be bound only, but also to die . . . . I am now ready to be offered . . . to me to die is gain."

A man who can so speak is invulnerable; the forces of this world cannot break such courage; no threats or violence can subdue such selfless faith. Paul has the world beaten! So the infant Church defied the rulers of Jerusalem: "Why did the heathen rage and the people imagine vain things? The kings of the earth stood up and the rulers were gathered together against the Lord and against his Christ . . ." but the Church well knew that in all their fierce hostility the men of might had only done "whatsoever God's hand and counsel had determined should be done". And Paul understood that at Calvary Christ had stripped off from Himself principalities and powers, triumphing over them, and at the Ascension He had been raised far above all principalities and powers, all might and dominion, and every name that is named on earth or in the heavens.

As these first believers saw it, at Calvary the world's power had over-reached itself, and stands exposed as weakness. The world's might arrayed against Jesus had crucified itself: for Jesus rose, and Paul — and all who share his faith — are unafraid.

And so it was with the world's allurement. This, too, was a direct danger to the infant Church. The young Christians were everywhere beset with sights and sounds, enticements and suggestions, of evil things. Immediately before using this striking phrase Paul has listed the works of the flesh that made the week's headlines in any Roman city. Elsewhere he could add "and such were some of you" and then as swiftly comment: "but ye are washed, ye are sanctified, and justified in the name of the Lord Jesus".

And this comment was true. For these young believers the old fascination of evil was broken. Seen from the brow of Calvary, the glittering world had lost all attractiveness, like some coarse and ugly fun fair when the lights are put out, the stalls deserted, the music subsides, and only the smell of dampness, the cheap vulgarity, assail the senses. Paul could not love the world that had crucified his Lord. In his eyes the whole brilliant façade of meretricious gilt and simulated pleasure lay exposed for sorry make-believe masquerading pathetically as happiness. It claimed indeed to "live": in fact it had put to death the Prince of Life.

So, though he would not hold aloof from the world's teeming

life, Paul would rise superior to it; not contemptuously, but as being delivered from it, and in order to improve it. He could "out-think, out-live, out-die" the world because he saw that it had crucified itself in crucifying Christ. He would neither boast its wisdom, fear its threats, nor succumb to its temptations: his whole passionate loyalty to Christ crucified lies behind that vigorous "God forbid!"

Christ was crucified for the sins of men: we are crucified with Christ: the world is crucified to us. Behold the Lamb of God, who thus completely taketh away the sin of the world!

12   Easter Exhortations

IT is not surprising that the gladness of the Easter faith and the glory of the risen Lord should somewhat distract attention from the plain and homely duties that arise from the Easter message. But exhortations — even commands — are clearly there, embedded in the story, and obedient hearts will not fail to hear them amid the beat of angels' wings, the rush of hurrying feet, the babble of excited, though fearful, voices, and the spreading hallelujahs of the joyful Church.

First, certainly, is the command to "come and see". The angels said it in the garden: Come, see the place where the Lord lay. Jesus echoed it that evening: Behold My hands and My feet, that it is I Myself; handle Me and see. And again a week later He said: Reach hither thy finger and behold My hands . . . . First see the place, empty; then the Lord, and no other; then know the finger-touch reality of personal contact. By such increasing degrees of certainty does the full resurrection faith come home to many men.

For the great truth of Easter is not equally vivid and compelling to all Christians. To some it is just the fit ending to the story; to others, an inference of faith; to yet others, a wistful hope. Some walk the road to Emmaus with Christ, their eyes holden; but for others the Easter message is the clearest fact of Christian faith, a glorious certainty, the shining centre from which all life — and death — borrow a radiant meaning.

And as with all gospel truth, the only way to know is to come and see. The only possible way to be sure is to meet the Master, to seek His presence, surrender to His claim, giving Him a chance to reveal Himself by accepting His own invitation to certainty: Come, and *see*.

Second is the exhortation, Be not afraid. The meeting of disciples behind locked doors is eloquent of the fear that kept them silent and sorrowing. The deep gloom of Calvary's eclipse was in their very souls! They knew the fear of the world's ruthless forces that seemingly had broken Him. They knew the fear of disillusion, lest their dreams and prayers should all prove vain. They felt the fear of the future, lest His glowing promises should come to nothing. They tasted already the fear of death — as He had died. And on that Easter morning, surrounded by miracles and wonders, they knew the still deeper, instinctive dread of a mysterious, unknown, other world, the superstitious fear that does not believe but cannot rest in unbelief.

We, too, have our fears; and we have learned the tragic power of fear to undermine the soul and betray reason itself. We know that fear of insecurity can threaten the growing child; that fear of life can produce a poisoning neurosis; that fear of God and death can ultimately destroy religious faith and peace. We moderns fear *fear* itself; and yet every discovery we make of the vastness and power of the universe about us makes us more afraid.

Against all doubt and dread Jesus sets the Easter confidence: faith in the resourcefulness of God; in the divine surprise of joy; in the wisdom and power of a God never baffled, defeated or outdone; in the basic friendliness to man of the unseen world and the eternal Father. The risen Christ still walks the world that sought to destroy Him and could not: Be not afraid!

If fears undermine, cynicism corrodes. The problem for

Thomas was the biting suspicion that all Christ stood for had been proved untrue, leaving a hard, unyielding doubt which put all good news, all uplifting truth, beyond belief. The obstinate questioning whether Christ had not misled them all or, even worse, had been Himself misled, in a world where Pilate and Caiaphas are the final realities and only the intolerable is likely to be true, turns very easily into the fatal mood that will not listen or learn but only declare, "I *will* not believe!"

A deep cynicism that suspects all good, all principles, all people, and believes only in evil, makes a desert of many modern souls, menacing all idealism, rejecting all standards, scoffing at all hope. The infection of a universal unbelief lends a smart veneer, a snobbish intellectual alibi, to mere licentiousness. Yet cynicism is a weak indulgence, a mental vice as truly as lust is an emotional one and avarice a moral one; and it fouls no less the springs of trust, of kindliness, of self-restraint and high endeavour.

But who can be cynical in a garden, in the morning, with the risen Lord? "Be not faithless!" — This is My Father's world, truth and love are still triumphant, life will conquer death. Hope on: hope still in God, in Christ, in truth, and in tomorrow — for Jesus lives.

The fourth duty facing us on Easter morning follows plainly from the other three. Go, tell His disciples, said the angels. Go, tell My brethren, said Jesus. Go to My brethren, was His word to Mary. Go ye into all the world, was His command to all. This is the most frequent Easter exhortation: Go quickly, Go your way, Go and tell. Indeed, there is not a single Easter story of the risen Lord which does not in some way embrace those to whom the news must come, those who shall hereafter believe, those whose faith is still to be nourished on the Easter truth.

It could not be otherwise, for in the Easter faith we have the antidote to the world's deep fears, an armour against the cynicism of men, a word for the ear of the race — a word of hope undefeated, of love unchanged, of salvation at hand, of a Lord reigning. Go and tell! for the world needs to hear, and only you *can* tell that

He who on the cross a Victim
For the world's salvation bled,
Jesus Christ, the King of glory,
Now is risen from the dead.

13 Ascensiontide

THOUGH probably the least observed of all the greater
Christian festivals, Ascensiontide is the true climax of the Christian year. Without its truth, Advent and Easter are incomplete;
faith, discipleship, experience and even ministry are, as we shall
see, impoverished. The comparative neglect of this joyous
anniversary may possibly arise from some uncertainty as to
what precisely the ascension adds to the Christian message. Or
it may be for want of a vivid and dramatic picture of what
happened that Ascensiontide grips the imagination less than do
Christmas or Good Friday.

Yet this is not altogether true. The last description of Jesus,
standing above the hill at Bethany, with hands upraised in
blessing over the disciples as He is parted from them, should
surely be familiar to Christian hearts. And beside it we may set
the representation of a Roman triumph, which lies behind much
of the New Testament's language concerning the ascension.

A victorious Roman commander, returning from some successful campaign, would lead his elated armies in procession
through the capital to the seat of Mars, to give thanks for victory. His cavalcade would be heralded by long lines of captives,
brought home as evidence of conquest, to be both slaves and spoil.
Following these would pass chariots laden with booty, from which
largesse for the populace, coins for the children, sometimes bribes
for the envious and suspicious politicians, would be freely distributed. The parade of standards, the martial songs, the fragrance of burning incense and trampled flowers, the pomp and

pride of great power released in jubilation, all made a Roman holiday.

Such was the developed Roman version of a very ancient custom. The centuries-old song of Barak tells of the train of captives, at once proof and reward of his great prowess. The Psalm of Jerusalem celebrates the entry of the Lord of Hosts at the head of His captive-train, giving (or it may be here, receiving) His lavish gifts. Isaiah promised that the Servant shall prolong His days, dividing His portion with the great and sharing the spoil with the strong. Roman practice and Old Testament language combine to lend force and drama to the great gospel affirmations concerning Jesus.

"God leadeth us in the train of his triumph, making manifest in every place the fragrance of knowing him; when he ascended up on high he led captive many captives and gave gifts unto men; being by the right hand of God exalted, he hath shed forth this; henceforth he expecteth until his enemies be made his footstool. . . ."

For faith, this means essentially that we serve a victorious Lord. Easter is full of His triumph over men and over death: the ascension extends the range of His victory to principalities and powers, the world-rulers of this darkness, powers of the height and depth — over the totality of opposing forces of all conceivable kinds.

The unfamiliarity of the language must not hide from us the timeless truth. Deliverance from demonic tyranny through the ascension of Christ was a most real and precious blessing of the gospel to first-century believers; and we still live in the sense of liberation which it brought to them. Christ is not still struggling for the world's unwilling recognition. He sits at God's right hand in regal majesty, far above *all* power and might and "every name that is named".

Looking back in grateful wonder to the incarnation, in humble thankfulness to the atonement, we must learn to look up more often in confidence and joyful anticipation to the priestly intercession and universal exaltation of "this same Jesus". He is *Christus Victor,* and His victory — wrought at Calvary, manifest

40

in the resurrection, acclaimed in the ascension — ought constantly to be reaffirmed in us, who are led in the train of His triumph.

But who are these who form His train, contributing to the splendour of His triumph, evidence and reward of His suffering and valour? They are His captives: Paul, the prisoner of Christ Jesus, bound with His chain and bearing in his body the slave-marks of the Lord Jesus; Peter, the bondslave of Christ; and all the rest of the apostolic Church, and of the long line of believers, warriors and heroes who follow in their train. These are Christ's inheritance in the saints, the spoils of His campaign, His captives; enlisted now, it is true, in His triumphant ranks, but first conquered and subdued by love to the willing acceptance of His mastery.

Here is a dimension of discipleship of which Ascensiontide ought constantly to remind us. We triumph in Christ, *provided that* He first has triumphed over us. We overcome, but no more and no less, and in no other way, than we are overcome by Him. Until we are wholly His, it cannot be *right* for us to rule; until we are wholly subdued, it cannot be *safe* for us to reign in life. He ascended to pre-eminence — over us.

"He shed forth this . . .", says Peter, embracing in a phrase the whole new wonder of Pentecost and linking it directly to Christ's ascending up on high. The Spirit of vision and of dreams, the Spirit of power and of conviction, the Spirit of tongues and of communication, the Spirit of joy, of divine intoxication, the Spirit of boldness and of fearlessness — all that Pentecost meant to the infant Church (and through the promise "to all them that are afar off" can mean also to us) is the gift of the enthroned Jesus to His own. This is the Conqueror's largesse, the sharing of the "spoils" of suffering and victory. So John also links the giving of the Spirit to the "glorifying" of the Lord.

Perhaps Pentecost would be easier to understand, as it certainly would mean more in our experience, if we approached its truth, not by searching wistfully and self-accusingly within our own frustrated hearts, but with our eyes upon Him, high and lifted up, His train filling the court of the heavenly temple,

41

and His love "shedding forth this" amazing gift, not as the reward for good behaviour, but in the shared, unselfish joy of His own glorious triumph.

". . . And gave gifts unto men, firstly apostles . . . prophets . . . pastors . . . teachers, for the work of the ministry." So runs another passage, still describing the bestowals of the ascended Lord. Yet how rarely we think thus of the Christian ministry — even we who are ministers. The authority of the minister, the quality, the preparation, the call, the unction, the consecration and message of the ministry, all are gifts of the glorified Christ to enrich His Church, gifts appointed in the joy of His exaltation. The festival of the Ascension has a great meaning, though a humbling one, for the servants of the King.

This is something constantly to be pondered by those whose hearts grow weary amid the tensions and conflicts, the perplexities and frustrations, of the ministry of the gospel. It must be borne in mind, too, by those who face the choice of a career and wonder if the work of the ministry is their vocation, and whether the discipline and sacrifice involved are worth their while. No earnest man will allow the sense of his call and ordination to foster pride; nor will any intelligent man seek to remind others, at any time, of his privileged position. But at times he will thank God, humbly, for putting him into the ministry, and be glad at heart, when the days are hard, to know that the ascended Lord gave the ministry to the Church. He will ponder anew each Ascensiontide the wonder of his own experience and call, and take up the work again with renewed patience, fresh zeal, and a surer hope.

14 "Not . . . But . . . ."

BY a curious coincidence, several New Testament references to God's gift of the Spirit fall into a similar pattern of expression: "God has not given us the spirit of . . . but . . . ." We might suppose this a mere idiosyncrasy of speech, if it were not that three instances are from Paul and the Pastoral Epistles, and the fourth, differently phrased but conveying a similar antithesis, is from John.

This suggests a deliberate and habitual contrast, familiar to the early Church, the gift of the Spirit being purposefully set over against certain tendencies or dangers already prevalent among Christians, and seen to be not just temporary phases of Christian development but inherent dangers of the new faith. The coincidence of language, in other words, may well be a symptom of a situation found to be repeating itself. It betrays a constant need to see the possession of the Spirit as God's appointed safeguard against recurring temptations that would beset Christians in all ages.

"We have received, not the spirit of the world, but the Spirit which is of God" suggests, for example, that the possession of the divine Spirit is the perpetual antidote to *worldliness*. At first sight, it might appear that excessive *other*-worldliness is the besetting peril of the Church, until one remembers how frequently Christians have forgotten that other world, and with great ingenuity and considerable success have come to terms with this.

The wealth, splendour, and pomp of the medieval Church is a measure of the spirit of the world within the Church; but so is the constant temptation, by no means always resisted, to frame the Christian message with an eye to the prevailing winds of opinion. We are so fearful of too narrow an emphasis. We want to show only the sweet reasonableness, the attractive breadth, of the Christian way, and present the gospel as a welfare prescription for adjusted, healthful, comforted living, rarely as the way of discipline, self-denial and sacrifice.

So, too, we tend to judge all statements of Christian truth and ethics by the measure in which they promise the bettering and reforming of this world, conducting to a greater sum of human *happiness*. Yet these are all essentially worldly, box-office standards of judgment. We have to live in this world, win this world, save this world, claim this world for God: yet we have always to remember that we are strangers and pilgrims, whose citizenship and whose treasure are in heaven. Only the Holy Spirit, Paul suggests, Representative of another world indwelling our lives within this world, can keep the balance true.

At the opposite pole is the perpetual temptation to reduce Christianity to yet another system of spiritual bondage. Extremes meet here. The ultra-Catholic builds his monasteries, raises his pillars, proclaims austerity and self-torture, sets his face resolutely against much that is healthy, natural, happy and free. The ultra-Evangelical has often an unwritten code of behaviour equally negative, cheerless, rigorous, and unlovely, denying to the Christian all joy in God's world, all delight in human love, all freedom, tolerance, gaiety and fun. Either exaggeration of the Christian discipline fetters the soul.

But "ye have not received the spirit of bondage . . . but ye have received the Spirit of adoption": the Spirit, that is, who testifies within us that we are sons of God endowed with the freedom of His family and His house. Whenever we are tempted to judge character by solemnity, depth of faith by lack of humour, making Christian life an obstacle race for fettered souls instead of a singing pilgrimage for newly liberated hearts, — *how* we need the Spirit of sonship, that joyously cries, "Abba, Father!" and stands fast in the liberty wherewith Christ has made us free!

Timothy is repeatedly warned against too timid an approach to the tasks of the ministry. So the disciples had been warned more than once against fearfulness — "Fear not, little flock . . . . Fear not them which kill the body . . . . Why are ye so fearful? . . ." John, too, insists that he that feareth is not made perfect in love, for love exorcises fear. Luke, again, underlines the boldness of Spirit-filled men like Peter and John.

"Be not afraid" is a constant exhortation which reveals that in the ancient Church as in the modern a sense of unworthiness, of insufficiency, of numerical insignificance, could daunt brave hearts; and the fallacy of imagination that makes us suppose noise, force, threats, publicity, horror, are stronger than truth, faith and love could breed a timid spirit. Yet "God has not given us a spirit of cowardice, but of divine power, of Christlike love, of a disciplined mind" — the three mightiest things in history. This is indeed the true and original meaning of the Spirit's best-loved name: "the Comforter" — the One who *fortifies*.

Like every teaching religion, Christianity has been often troubled by a multitude of intellectual divisions, and frequently the truth has been lost in the contentions of its defenders. The gospel is a profound faith, life a complicated business; the denials of the enemy are subtle and contradictory; and Christians are not always amongst the most wise, well-educated, thoughtful. Yet the way to wisdom is the way of simple obedience, and "He has not given us the Spirit of error"! For all we need to know, God has promised us understanding; for all we need to learn, the Spirit of truth to guide each teachable mind. He does not promise omniscience, or infallibility: but the indwelling light of the Spirit will show us our way forward, if we are willing to learn.

However we may explain it, Christianity would seem to have been ever open to just these distortions and distractions. Perhaps because it is realistic, its feet firmly on the earth, keeping close to experience and aiming at God's kingdom in this world, the Church must reckon with the danger of becoming too concerned with this worldly realm. Perhaps because of its strongly ethical flavour, its lofty vision of the good life, its disciplined passion for Jesus, the gospel will ever tend to slip over into legalism and moral bondage. Perhaps just because Christians possess so noble a conception of God, so deep a sense of sin, and make so direct a challenge to the world's will to persecute, there will always be some who give way to weakening distrust and fear. Perhaps because the message is a *faith*, an intellectual code interpreting nature and history in the light of good *news* in Christ, there will always be the peril of misunderstanding and heresy.

The dangers might be said to be inherent in the nature of the gospel. But He who has foreseen the perpetual temptations has given us His abiding Spirit, the prophylactic against worldliness and bondage, against fear and error — the divine Greatheart whose task and joy it is to succour every pilgrim on the King's highway.

45

15 The Strong Name

THE things a man must know in order to be saved are mercifully few and simple. But who wants to live on bare necessities? The cult of simple, untheological, man-in-the-street-to-man-in-the-pew religion is unworthy of the hearer: for the complexities and paradoxes with which many wrestle today in physics, technology, tax-assessments and pool-betting would leave most theologians standing! It is equally unworthy of the magnificence of the gospel, and inevitably shallow thinking and superficial teaching make for impoverished faith and beggarly experience. The Christian's creed has depths to swim in, and it is nothing to boast about if we have never plunged in over our ankles.

Then thank God for Trinity Sunday!

Those who profess impatience with the mystery of the Trinity may find it hard to believe that (in the words of one authority) the Trinitarian conception is implied in Christian thinking from the start, and (according to another) is stated between seventy and eighty times in the New Testament. So much for the original, untheological simplicities of the early faith!

Here indeed is no invention of word-spinning theorists complicating needlessly a plain and winsome idyl. Here rather is the Church reverently drawing together the threads of her thought about God and striving to express her faith in one great declaration commensurate with her experience: "We believe in one God, Father, Son, and Holy Spirit."

That is why Trinity Sunday could only follow Advent, Epiphany, Lent and Easter, Ascension and Pentecost; for so the Church had reached her faith. Men trained in the Hebrew creed knew God as Creator, Lord of nature, history and conscience; and they learned of Jesus to add the gentler title, Kingly Father, which art in heaven.

But in Christ Himself they had found God nearer, and accessible, shorn of majesty and outward glory but with unmistakably divine power dwelling within Him, divine truth speaking through Him, divine grace flowing out of Him. They already believed in God, now they believed also in Christ.

Then had come Pentecost, and something they had recognised in Christ, the Source of eternal truth and power and love, now manifested itself in the life of the Church, dwelling even within themselves: and this, too, they knew to be divine — no lesser definition would do. How could men with such experience attempt to say all they meant by "God" without thinking of Father, Son, and Spirit?

We, too, look out at a breath-takingly majestic and mysterious universe, and think of God. We look back at the career, the character, the cross of Jesus, and think of God. We look within our own inexplicable experience as sinners redeemed and kept by something not ourselves, and we think of God. It is not only that

> Some Seek a Father in the heavens above,
> Some ask a human image to adore;
> Some crave a Spirit vast as life and love —
> Within Thy mansions we have all — and more:

it is that *all* need *the whole* of God; and in the Christian revelation we have found a glorious Godhead, Source and Sustainer of an adequate, everlasting salvation.

This relation of theology to experience makes especially appropriate the invocation of the Strong Name of the Trinity at the great moments of the Christian life. At baptism, for example, when we acknowledge the love of the Father who spared not His own Son but delivered Him up for us all; the sacrifice of the Son, our Redeemer and Master, Saviour and Lord; the inward conviction and regenerating power of the Spirit who shows men themselves and shows them their Saviour. Omit either emphasis — the originating love, the mediating sacrifice, or the regenerating Spirit — and Christian conversion is at once incomplete, Christian assurance is weakened, Christian discipleship limps. We are baptised in the Triune Name because only so is the fullness of our salvation truthfully expressed.

So is it at the Supper. Here especially do we "through *Christ* have access by one *Spirit* unto the *Father*". Here we recall with

47

gratitude God's pardoning love, for the feast is a giving of thanks. Here we remember the Source and the price of our redemption, for the feast is a memorial and an expectation of the Saviour Christ. Here we reaffirm our fellowship in the Spirit of the risen Lord, for the feast is an act of communion, too. Again the threefold emphasis is essential to completeness of experience: to omit either truth is to miss something of the divine intention.

And could anything be more fitting than that, at the end of an epistle or at the close of a meeting, we should be set upon our way with the Strong Name in our ears? With the *grace of the Lord Jesus* to lend beauty and radiance, fragrance and joy, to all our journeying; with *the love of God* to provide and protect, to comfort and to kindle courage; with the *communion of the Holy Spirit* to illumine, direct, purify, empower — how can we travel otherwise than hopefully, or doubt that under the blessing of the Triune God we shall triumphantly arrive?

16 God Hidden

V ERILY thou art a God that hidest thyself!" How could any Biblical writer say such a thing? Scripture's central emphasis flatly contradicts it. From the first poetic picture of God walking with Adam to the final vision of the New Jerusalem descending out of heaven that God might dwell with men, the underlying message of Biblical faith is that God comes forth out of the mystery and isolation of eternity to seek men, meet men, walk with men.

Throughout the history of Israel men saw the hand of God at work, the heart of God laid bare. God had spoken. The essential promise of the Old Testament is that "the Lord shall come"; the essential news of the New Testament is that the Word became flesh and dwelt among us.

How then can any prophet say, Thou hidest Thyself?

If this were a solitary, exceptional outburst, one might pass it lightly by: but it is echoed otherwhere. One Psalmist asks, in doubt, How doth God know, and is there knowledge in the Most High? Another answers, in despair, God hath forgotten — He hideth His face! Job cries in anguish, Oh, that I knew where I might find Him; Eliphaz declares that God is too high to know or judge: "What can the Almighty do?"

Even in the New Testament echoes are heard of this complaint about the divine elusiveness. There is stress and shadow in the soul of Paul as he writes II Corinthians: faintheartedness and loss of faith have to be dealt with among the Hebrew Christians, while throughout the later pages the call is to hold fast and hold out in testing days when God seems far away.

In the manuals of spiritual discipline of the Middle Ages, the dark night of the soul, "the time of arid dryness and great darkness", was a recognised stage in spiritual development. And Bunyan, for all his blessed assurance, makes Christian walk through the valley of humiliation and great darkness.

God, it is certain, delighteth to make Himself known; yet there is an experience, familiar to the saints, of the hiding of His face. It is good to realise, when the experience comes upon you, that others have been where you now are, and have lived to see again the sunlight of God's smile. So will you.

But it is essential to remember that the hiding of God's face is most frequently our own fault, arising from a heart out of fellowship, a soul out of tune, a life out of alignment. "If I regard iniquity in my heart, the Lord will not hear me" is one of the shrewdest scriptural insights; "If we say we have fellowship with him and walk in darkness, we lie" is one of the most honest self-judgments; "Hide thy face from my sins" is a most understanding prayer.

This turning away of God's face *in disapproval* may well be in the mind of the Exile prophet. The sin of Judah has brought her into the darkness of punishment, the awful, desolating fear of banishment. Always the cure is plain. To the plea "Where is the blessedness I knew?" there can be only one reply —

> *The dearest idol I have known,*
> *Whate'er that idol be,*
> *Help me to tear it from Thy throne*
> *And worship only Thee.*

But if sin were always the explanation, there would be no problem: cause and consequence would belong obviously together. The prophet has more in mind. The hand and power of God were hard to discern in the years when Israel's heathen captors appeared invincible and permanent, the future hopeless. But on the horizon of the chapter stands Cyrus, who shall break Babylon and reverse her policies. Egypt, too, and Ethiopia shall know God's power and Israel's glory. The future, after all, is bright!

Who would have thought, in the bitterness of these long years of punishment and defeat, that God was still at work for Israel? "Verily thou art a God that hidest thyself!" There is a hiding of His face *in discipline* of faith: the Lord delights to prepare His rosiest dawn in the darkest night, and to surprise His children with unexpected, and unlooked-for, deliverance. If God seems hid, that by no means proves He is not there.

But there is another hiding of God's face, that arises not from sin, or lack of insight, but simply from the fact that He is God. It is one thing to believe that God is His own interpreter and He will make it plain; it is perhaps a higher faith that realises that God is His own master, too, and may not choose to make it plain.

About one particular matter Jesus said, "God hath hid these things." About another, "No man knoweth, neither the Son...." About a third, "It is not for you to know". And about yet a fourth, "What I do thou knowest not now".

With words like these before us, surely only irreverence demands to know all God's reasons; as only an immature, clamorous faith will claim to understand all God's dealings with His children. Humility, and mature trust, are content with darkness if the Father so appoints, sure that if He hides His face His heart is not turned from us. We can walk on, bereft sometimes of consolation but never forsaken of God, until He shall please to lift upon us again the light of His countenance and give us once more His peace.

17 Rock and Pit

I T is, of course, always important to notice to whom a scripture passage is addressed, and in what circumstances. Isaiah 51 is for those who pursue after righteousness, hungering and thirsting for the victory of right: the idealists and the men of faith who seek first God's kingdom. But the time is the Exile, when the cause of right (in Jewish eyes) was in eclipse and the future foreboding if not hopeless.

In such a time, counsels the prophet, men of understanding will look to the past, to the rock whence they were hewn and the pit whence they were digged. They will recall the small beginnings of Israel, the apparently hopeless start, when God called one man to leave Ur — one solitary soul against a generation. But they will remember that the one became a family, a clan, a nation, a race. From one, as good as dead, had arisen a multitude "as sand upon the sea shore".

There is thus no forecasting God's success, no keeping up with His multiplication table. As with the solitary Abraham, so shall it be with the tiny remnant returning from Exile. What God has done He still can do. Look back, marvel at what the Lord hath done, and take heart for tomorrow!

Such is the prophet's essential argument: but the backward glance is here characterised in a particular way. "Look to the *rock* whence ye were hewn, to the *pit* whence ye were digged." In this connection, "rock" is a complimentary term, suggesting endurance, usefulness, strength, dependability. Israel has proved to be God's rock amidst the drifting sand of the nations, the one enduring people tenacious of her faith and destiny while empires rise and fall around her. And Abraham was the one small quarry, so to speak, from which Israel had been hewn.

This is the appeal, familiar in the later Old Testament, to the distant past as the source of all that is best in the nation's life. "Return to the old ways, the former paths, the stopped wells that once refreshed your fathers .... Return!" Look to the rock of your origins, and remember the factors that created your strength and endurance: the faith and obedience of Abraham, the centuries of toughening and education through judges, kings and prophets. Remember how much you owe to those who went before you and made you what you are. Hold a Thanksgiving Day for yesterday!

That is a hard word for us, who like to trace our weaknesses and problems, our sins and incapacities, to those who went before us, and look back in anger: but our virtues, our daring, our discoveries and scientific genius to our own courage and "the modern spirit". It is a comfortable attitude, but entirely self-deceptive. Alike in intellect and spirit we are heirs of all the ages: it is but good sense and simple justice to hold a grateful day of remembrance in honour of those whose thought and labour created our opportunities and bequeathed to us our new capacities. Especially in the richer aspects of experience are we unpayably in debt to those whose friendship, witness, faithfulness and prayers helped to make us whatever we are that is worth while.

But if "rock" is complimentary, the word "pit" has very different implications; and to make this plainer the prophet says "that hole of a pit". Three associations of the pit in Old Testament thought are mud, dungeons, and the grave. The images conjured up are those of rescue from a horrible fate beneath the miry clay; of man's helplessness and mortality, and God's delivering mercy. If we do well to keep in mind the quarry of God's grace from which, through parents, church, ministry, experience, love has hewed us, we do well equally to recall the pit from which we were mercifully redeemed, the mire from which we had to be saved.

Can it be accidental that these two ideas are here so closely linked? Israel in exile needed *both* an awareness of the great possibilities within her, lest she despair of ever serving God again, and a true sense of her sinfulness and need. Remembrance of the deep truths she had learned, the great things God had done, the glorious destiny for which she had been prepared, would stimulate her hope and confidence. But remembrance of her fault and failure would teach the deeper lessons — equally necessary — of penitence, humility and grace. Both rock and pit are in every man's experience, and neither may be forgotten by the grateful, healthy soul.

52

The rich meaning of religious experience can scarcely be better summarised than in these two words. The prophet cannot have had in mind all their wide suggestiveness, but he is using familiar and far-ranging terms that run through scripture, gathering deep significance on their way. *Rock* belongs to a group of metaphors that sees Israel as a "house", God as the supreme Architect, the nation "built" by divine wisdom. Later Christ is the foundation, the believers are living stones elect and precious, each fitly framed to rise together a shrine for God's indwelling through the Spirit. This is the godly man's experience seen, as it were, from the outside: the shaping of his soul by providence and discipline to fit with others in the eternal Temple.

But *pit*, and the clay dug therefrom, recalls the Potter's art, and the divine workmanship that within the soul shapes vessels for the Master's use. Man's helplessness in the Potter's hands, and the everlasting patience that will begin again if the work be marred, are the truths enshrined. Here is the godly man's experience seen from the inside, the transformation of the soul by mercy, tenderness and redeeming grace.

Material for God's building, clay in God's hands — here are clues to the meaning of religious experience that illumine every backward look and move us constantly to thanksgiving.

18 Things Not Seen

THE eleventh chapter of Hebrews opens with the startlingly honest admission that faith does not always obtain the things it hoped for, nor live to see accomplished the things that inspired its dream. The point is reiterated with remarkable emphasis through the chapter. Noah was warned of things not seen, Abraham lived in expectation of a land and a city he never inherited. Sarah saw Isaac, but not the fulfilled purpose of

Isaac's birth. We are expressly told that these all died in faith, *not* having received the promises.

Isaac blessed Jacob and Esau concerning the unseen future, and Joseph's dying commandment looked forward through four hundred years. Moses strove, and suffered, and sacrificed, but saw not the land of promise except from afar. Joshua never saw the campaign finished, the nation's life established; David never lived to gaze upon the Temple.

Prophets, leaders, warriors and saints wandered, were tempted, were persecuted, suffered and died in faith, "not having received the promises" — the phrase is repeated! To them all, faith gave substance to the things they hoped for, but which never came within their grasp; it was its own best evidence of things they did not live to see.

This is not how we usually speak of faith. We claim faith gains the victory; we recite its fine accomplishments, its answers to prayer, its great occasions. We give personal testimony to amazing coincidences, exciting experiences, special providences. We all have our treasured memories of God's doing this, or providing that, or arranging the other thing, in answer to our cry. "Faith dares impossibilities and cries, 'It shall be done!'"

All this is true, or should be. Abraham, Moses, Joshua at Jericho, David and the rest have much to tell of the things in which faith was wondrously rewarded, and the hand of God was seen. Certainly God does great things for those who trust Him, and we are poorer than we need be, less blessed, less steadfast than we should be, more perplexed, more timid and more frustrated than we have any right to be, because we do not know enough of these individual providences, heart-moving deliverances and answers to prayer, that God promises and faith obtains.

On the whole we are probably a generation of men of little faith, needing often to pray, "Lord, I believe, help thou mine unbelief". We are more partial to welfare and security than to walking in the darkness with our hand in God's. Perhaps we have some excuse in the temper of our time and the long-ebbing tide of spiritual life that we have had to row against. But God's promises are sure, and timeless. All things are still possible to him that believeth, and there is awaiting every Christian an endless discovery of new powers and opportunities, new resources and illumination, if our faith can match God's faithfulness, and our hearts move out of unbelieving Nazareth, where little can be done, on to Cana, where the disciples believed on Him and water was turned to wine.

Even so, this experience of the faith that gets, satisfying and exciting though it is, nevertheless is not faith at its deepest level, putting forth its noblest strength. It is but elementary beside the faith that has learned to ask and go without. Such was Mary's, as she waited for Jesus when Lazarus lay dying, and waited in vain. Her reward was the promise, "Said I not unto thee, that if thou wouldest believe thou shouldest see the glory of God?"

Such, too, was the truly heroic faith of the three who defied the Babylonian king: "Our God is able to deliver us, *but if not*, know that we will not bow . . . ." It is the quality of faith that can add to the grateful "The Lord gave . . ." the courageous "The Lord hath taken away: blessed be the name of the Lord".

The two outstanding "unanswered" prayers of the New Testament ("ungranted" would be the truer word) illustrate the same point: the prayer of Jesus in Gethsemane and the prayer of Paul concerning his thorn in the flesh are alike prayers of superb faith denied the things it asks. And on a slightly different level, but still relevant — who can forget the deaths of Stephen and James, martyred so soon, before the rich promise of their lives could be fulfilled? So very many have died in faith, not having received the promise by which they lived.

And this, let us not forget, would seem to be the experience of a great number whose faith and dedication are not in doubt, but who travelled hopefully without seeming to arrive, and strove heroically without appearing to achieve. Spiritual development advances from the unbelief that never asks, and is needlessly impoverished, to the faith that asks and gets, finding God true, *and then on* to the faith that asks and goes without, and yet is richer, stronger and at greater peace because it has learned to let God have His way. Such mature souls have learned that faith is itself the substance of the things it hoped

55

for, the evidence in their own experience of things longed
for but as yet withheld.

19 Slippers

MOST parents now at middle age will long remember the
period when "no corporal punishment at any price" was the first
rule of child-training; when a smack was a major social barbarism,
and to admit to an occasional beating was to confess abysmal
psychological ignorance and appalling parental incompetence.
Whatever the effects upon the children, the wear and tear of
parents and teachers was enormous. But now that the consequences for society begin to be obvious, the theories conveniently
change.

Parents are listening with wry interest to the shuffle of the
slipper's return as an instrument of education. Child psychology
is rediscovering the need for discipline "judiciously applied".
Schoolmasters, court officials, probation officers, and even higher
authorities engage yet again in the familiar pastime of lecturing
parents, but this time on the need for *not* giving in, for not
granting all that is demanded, and for occasionally imprinting
a notion of right and wrong upon the seat of character with a
firm hand upon the slipper-heel.

The swing of the pendulum apart, and the real danger of
parental bullying notwithstanding, it is high time that theoretical
psychology was wedded to some plain horse-sense in dealing with
childish mischief that is healthy enough in itself but which
needs to be checked at recognised boundaries. Too often mere
naughtiness is exaggerated by fatuous definitions into "psychic
maladjustment", "anti-social delinquency trends" and all the
rest: while at the other extreme we near the point where no one
may claim protection in our modern society except the proved
bully, criminal, or rebel.

So much is obvious. But one wonders if at long last a much
deeper lesson may not be waiting us: whether indeed the note

of moral rigour may not soon be sounded again in theology and religion, the accent of moral sternness be recovered in the training of disciples, and with it the manliness and strength of character which a just, consistent sternness often breeds.

Three men in scripture owed success to the sternness of their mentors. David possesses much that endears him to faith: youthful charm, a soldier's bravery, poetry, and the glamour of outlaw adventuring combine with his place in the ancestry of Christ to make him favorite among Old Testament characters long after Sunday-school days. Yet David sinned, grievously, tyrannically, dirtily. While his penitence was likewise great, it was to the courage and forthright sternness of Nathan that David owed forgiveness, and that we owe David.

Every consideration of personal safety, public peace, royal prerogative and human frailty might have argued defence of the king, or at least a diplomatic silence. Nathan's "Thou art the man!" is the banner of every unintimidated conscience, and the measure of that loyalty to truth and honour that puts faithfulness to another's soul above moral laziness, fear of unpopularity, want of conviction, or selfish, cynical indifference.

John Mark made a grievous mistake, born of a narrow mind, or fear, or just the waning of enthusiasm; and for it he forfeited the company of Paul and the splendid opportunities of the second missionary journey. Barnabas was gentler, and granted the second chance that revealed Mark's quality and retrieved his whole career from ruin.

Of course, as the outcome showed and Paul himself later admitted by calling Mark "profitable", Barnabas was right. *But so was Paul.* It took both sternness at the hands of Paul and compassion in the heart of Barnabas to remake Mark. Paul, doubtless, will always be criticised by the sentimental hedonists who want to make Christian character the easy way; but there is little doubt that Mark himself would confound Paul's critics and confess that the warrior-apostle's firmness put iron into his soul.

Peter, as every schoolboy knows, stands out among the Twelve as one whom Jesus totally transformed. A study of Christ's method with this boisterous, impulsive, erring follower at once reveals the place of sternness in the development of great souls. Were ever sharper words addressed to man than Peter heard at Caesarea? "Get thee behind me, Satan. Thou savourest not the things that be of God, but those that be of men." Peter's boast, "Lo, we have left all . . ." is as quickly checked with the blunt reminder that no one leaves anything behind for Christ without more than adequate repayment. The impulsive apostle is forewarned of danger, but is not exempt the test that leads him to denial.

In the garden, Peter alone is rebuked; in the judgment hall the glance that brought Peter to tears was not compounded all of excusing pity and defence. At the lakeside he is made, gently but very, very firmly, to retrace his wayward steps: he stands again beside "a fire of coals", he is piercingly reminded that once he professed to love "more than these", he is directed to erase his threefold denial with a threefold confession of love. The old name is used -- "Simon, son of Jonas" -- as though the new "Peter" were held for a time in abeyance: and the scene ends with a deliberate return to the point where Peter long ago had begun with Christ, standing beside the lake after another miraculous draught of fish and hearing Jesus say to him, "Follow me!"

Not once in the record of Christ's dealings with this man is the foolish word or ill-considered deed allowed to pass. Always the keynote is the loving strength that means to make men strong. And the result, an unstable, emotional soul steeled to endurance, fired with a consuming passion for Christ, and forged at last to martyrdom.

There is something to be learned here of the nature of God, of the nature of man, of the nature of true love, and of pastoral psychology. The weak appeal, and weaker discipline, that has stemmed from the defensive situation of the Church in recent years has not made for loyal, virile membership. A sterner approach to social and moral issues, a higher Christian discipline for applicants, and a clearer obligation laid upon disciples might well develop again that better understanding of the law which conditions the mind for fuller appreciation of the gospel.

20 Spiritual Ambition

IT is customary to criticise sharply the request of James and John for seats beside Christ in His kingdom. There was, we think, in such a plea something strangely out of harmony with the mood of the last journey to Jerusalem; and something selfish, almost underhanded, in thus attempting to over-reach their brethren. The preamble to the request, too, sounds very presumptuous: "Master, we would that Thou shouldest do for us whatsoever we desire" — though we must confess that our own prayers are often on that basis. And we fancy there must be something worldly and materialist about any such ambition for pre-eminence in the kingdom. All in all it seems a sorry incident.

Yet Jesus Himself offered none of these criticisms. His "Ye know not what ye ask" is no rebuke for asking. Instead, Jesus makes a solemn and profound reply, some ten verses long, treating very seriously this matter of greatness in His kingdom. Here are two looking-ahead, going-ahead disciples, who do not believe that their present experience and attainment are all that Christ intended. If the request is crudely framed, it is nevertheless a genuine expression of spiritual restlessness, of ambition to get somewhere in discipleship, of a stirring desire for something better, some real achievement in Christian life.

And in this light, they speak in some measure for us all.

Such a mood of spiritual ambition seems to be stirring within the Church again in our day: a restless hunger for something more satisfying than dogged loyalty, more spectacular than merely holding on. Perhaps the causes of restlessness are not always very deep: dwindling numbers, losses among youth, unhappy divisions, financial strain, denominational rivalry, disappointment with results of zealous and proficient campaigns. Perhaps the expressions of this spiritual hunger are not altogether impressive: much self-criticism and endless fact-finding enquiries, panic experimentation with liturgies, techniques, and even doctrines, a mood of faultfinding and despondency. Even so, beneath it all there lies a true desire to get on, a wish to sit again in the seats of power within society, to *get somewhere* for Christ, to see something happen that will disturb the lethargy of the Church and startle the indifference of the world. Sometimes, too, a personal contact with an outstanding Christian, or an individual experience exposing our own poverty of faith, will stir the soul to new spiritual ambition and inward restlessness.

Jesus, surely, would not rebuke the awakening desire, or merely criticise the ways in which we blunderingly express it. But would He perhaps say to us what He said to James and John: "Ye know not what ye ask"?

What *do* we want? In this realm, vagueness is frequently the enemy of ambition and the mother of much frustration. A general return to the churches in their present divided, confused, and sometimes despondent state might not be at all a good thing. Certainly we are fooling ourselves if we suppose that larger congregations in themselves would provide the answer to the world's great problems or society's present perils. A vigorous, apostolic revival in the second half of this century might well have consequences — in the organisation and in the thought and practice of the churches — that we little dream of, and perhaps would little want.

What do we want? A Church more pure, or puritan? A Church more powerful, politically — or in what way? And if it seems obvious that we must desire a Church united, it is far from clear to what pattern that united Church must be designed. Do we, again, wish to see a Church more popular and influential, more at home in the world and integrated with common life — or a Church more plainly distinguished from the world, less compromising and more persecuted?

And what manner of Christians do we want to be? Less confused and far more confident, certainly; but do we wish to be less deeply involved in the complicated problems of our age, less concerned with the suffering around us? Do we envisage a discipleship more surely guided of God, more joyful, more busy and successful in Christian service, more useful in commonplace daily ways to folk about us — or just easier, happier, and less demanding?

It is far easier to ask than to answer such questions: but the truth is that ignorant, ill-formed, undirected spiritual ambition must remain unfulfilled. "Ye know not what ye ask" explains very often our failure to get it.

But Jesus' reply clearly means also, "Ye know not what it costs". For one thing, the two disciples thought that advancement in the kingdom was to be had for the asking. In fact, there are few things in spiritual life which are granted *merely* in answer to prayer.

For another thing, they forgot that pre-eminence in Christ's kingdom means pre-eminence in obedience and in service — it is that kind of kingdom. And so it must involve, as Jesus immediately says, a cup of sacrifice, a baptism of conflict, even as He Himself would crown His service by giving His life a ransom for many. The important spiritual endowments *can* only be given to those prepared to have them.

Are we prepared, then, for the fulfilment of our spiritual ambitions? Restless, hungry for greater blessing, are we ready for the price that must be paid? What might revival cost us in lost complacency, or in new responsibilities — or in difficult new entanglements over racial or nuclear policies? What wholesale changes of method, beliefs, ideas, and treasured traditions might not be involved if the wind of the Spirit really blew through our corporate Christian life! What would revival cost in holiness? or clearer guidance, greater power and fuller success cost us individually in readier obedience, disturbing zeal and yet more painful concern for men?

"Ye know not what ye ask": the need is for education in spiritual goals, by thought, analysis, self-knowledge, scripture; and then for honest assessment of the depth of our desire. For until we know what we want, and what we will pay for it, our spiritual hunger must go unsatisfied. We shall remain just restless, *merely* ambitious.

21 Discouragement

A surprising number of discouraged people appear in the gospel stories. The Baptist hears in prison strange things about Jesus and, puzzled and despondent, wonders if He can be the Christ. A sick woman pushes through the crowd in a last desperate effort to find health after many failures. The man by the pool of Bethesda seems too sorry for himself to make any longer the effort to seek a cure, and Peter retails to Jesus the story of a night's fruitless fishing, to show how pointless it is to try again.

With disappointment in their hearts the disciples watch the Galilean crowds dwindle, until Jesus startles their gloom with His "Will ye also go away?" Mary sits sad and hopeless in the house, and greets Jesus with a reproachful, "Lord, if thou hadst been here . . . ". The look of shocked dismay on the face of Jairus when news reaches him of his daughter's death makes Jesus "answer" it (as Luke says) with immediate assurance. And who can forget the two disheartened men going homewards through the twilight to Emmaus?

Not everyone has earned the right to be discouraged. But these had. John had preached courageously; the sick woman had spent all her living upon cures; the paralysed had waited forty years; Peter had fished all night. The disciples had left so much, Mary had waited so bravely, Jairus had pleaded so hard, the Emmaus disciples had hoped so earnestly that Jesus was Messiah. Yet each is despondent, discouraged, doubting: not, as sometimes happens, through laziness and spiritual sloth, but because of true hope long deferred, sincere effort unrewarded.

Discouragement is a miserable mood, and very dangerous. The impatient discouragement of the people time and again made the desert journey wearier with murmuring and complaint, and added forty unnecessary years to their wilderness wandering. The faithless discouragement of the spies nearly cost Israel its opportunity of Canaan. The frightened discouragement of Elijah made him flee from Jezebel to idle Horeb, and wish for himself that he might die. The self-pitying discouragement of

Gideon almost blinded him to the personal challenge of his time.

All this discouragement does, besides hiding from us the face of God. It defeats and disarms us when there are battles to be fought. It burdens us with complaints against our day and against our fellow workers. It plunges us into moody idleness when there is work waiting to be done. It kindles the futile longing for a return of old and better times. Feeding upon itself, it can always discover reasons to justify its gloom. And it is terribly infectious. The danger in discouragement is manifold and insidious: it demands a vigilant spirit.

How then did Jesus deal with this perilous sickness of the soul? His methods were varied. The disheartened disciples were given the parable of the sower, to help them understand hard facts about the hearts of men and *why* the crowds were dwindling. The Emmaus pair received a Bible-class exposition of the prophecies of a *suffering* Messiah. It is wonderful what a little reasonable explanation will do to dispel the black mood of despondency. Discouragement is so much an emotional indulgence that a common-sense assessment of a situation becomes almost impossible: but when some wise counsellor begins to analyse and interpret, how quickly things regain proportion.

Recall the fierce assaults that the faith has already outlived. Ponder and weigh seriously the factors that were ranged against the gospel when Paul set out from Antioch, Luther from his cell, Carey sailed for India, and Wesley began his work. Indeed, consider afresh the audacity of the Christian venture — to revolutionise the world; remember the towering challenge which the Church presents to men; measure afresh the inevitable scandal of the cross. Faced with such "handicaps", can the Church hope to be "popular"? — yet think how she has survived and what she has accomplished. It is useless of course to gloss over disquieting facts, but it is equally stupid to let emotional discouragement distort one's judgement.

In other cases Jesus offered not explanation but power. He reintroduced into forbidding situations the new, or forgotten, factor of the might of God. The sick woman, the daughter of Jairus, the paralysed man, Lazarus — each illustrates the incoming of an energy which the discouraged heart had failed to count upon. "Said I not unto thee that if thou wouldest believe thou shouldest see the glory of God?"

So very often, when we are busy estimating the probabilities of success — or survival — we minister to our own despondency by leaving God out of our reckoning. God is greater than all our statistics; and He is the hardest Fact in every situation. We cannot change hearts, or control events, or sustain the Church, or initiate revival — but God can. The tides of the Spirit are under His control. Oftener still we invite defeat by attempting great things without expecting great things, and without putting ourselves in the way to receive them.

To the Baptist in prison Jesus sent the counsel to look again at the signs of God's activity, and a recital of the things that were happening all about him in Israel. These were not what John had anticipated would happen when Messiah came; but the explanation was not that God was absent, but that John's expectations were wrong. We are reminded of Elijah, sharply rebuked for thinking himself the only loyal Israelite left, when seven thousand had not bowed the knee to Baal — a large number for a prophet not to notice! So, too, Jesus bade the Twelve lift up their eyes and see the fields white unto harvest — when they thought the ground parched, unyielding and barren.

Undoubtedly many things we would like to see happening are not taking place, but he who cannot see any sign of the Spirit's work in our time has allowed discouragement to cloud his discernment. Prodigious sales of the scriptures in countless translations; the new emphasis upon religious education and literacy; a deepening sense of the emptiness and danger of scientific materialism; a spreading concern for the moral and social consequences of irreligious youth; a deep and widespread theological awakening throughout the Church; an insistent demand for unity of witness; recognition on all hands that material welfare needs spiritual enrichment; the upsurge of the younger Churches, vigorous, joyous, and free — who can see such things and doubt that this, too, is God's time?

To others, again, Jesus gave something to do. Peter lets down the net again; the paralysed takes up his bed; someone opens the tomb, and later unrolls the gravecloths; the disciples are sent on their mission; even Jairus must prepare a meal; and the two fly from Emmaus to Jerusalem to bring the glad tidings. So Gideon had been sent to act against the Midianites as the divine cure for his despondency; so Elijah was given an urgent threefold task to drive him from Horeb and from despair.

For idleness breeds discouragement; and disobedience fosters it. Whatever your feelings, obey; however discouraged, keep right on with what is right. There is absolutely no need for you to provide by your own betrayal still further evidence of the decay you deplore! The truth is still true, what is right is right, — and God remaineth.

22 Thou Shalt Worship

OUT of the mists of the distant past, from beside a thousand ancient shrines and wayside altars, expressed in a multitude of differing rites and customs, comes the precept: Thou shalt worship. There speaks within it the accumulated wisdom of many generations; behind it lie the deepest instincts of the human spirit. But for us, the command gains authority through Moses, with the solemn reminder clearly implied in the Second Commandment, that gods we cease to worship soon cease to be gods to us. And that authority is immeasurably reinforced when Jesus quotes the words within the wilderness in the hour of His temptation. Custom, need, law and gospel unite to underline the counsel: Thou shalt worship.

But though the need, and the wisdom to meet it, be permanent, prevailing modern attitudes tend to obscure both. Modern life demands haste, for we live by schedules and time-signals: worship takes time, to attune the spirit and quieten the mind. Modern life demands aggressiveness: worship requires, perhaps above all else, humility, receptiveness and appreciation. Life nowadays is deeply controversial, calling for argumentative minds: worship requires of us the *listening* ear, and the *accepting* conscience.

Modern life is complicated, and we are conditioned to the tortuous approach to things: worship on the other hand demands simplicity, the direct and sincere spirit. On the whole we are probably far more extravert than our fathers, more deeply interested in the world outside ourselves than by the world within: worship involves some measure of honest and disciplined introspection.

Perhaps most difficult of all, the modern world accepts a man largely at his own valuation, so that success almost depends upon efficient "self-promotion". Worship, at the other extreme, requires *prostration* — not merely honest self-assessment, but awareness of one's creaturehood, frailty and mortality, deepened by penitence for *one's own* sins, and expressed in the actual bowing down of mind, conscience and will before the Most High. There may be deep psychological and even moral reasons why fewer and fewer people seem to *kneel* in prayer!

For very many, these general difficulties are intensified by the industrial context of their lives. The tone and atmosphere of countless working days are determined by the noise and stress, the speed and essential materialism, of mechanised and repetitive forms of employment. It is not only the dyer's hand and the miner's scars that bear the impress of particular types of toil: the inner personality is no less conformed to the materials it works in, the mental and spiritual habit of eight (or six!) hours each day.

It needed a novelist, probably, to remind us forcibly that the artist and the craftsman possess intuitive understanding of creatorhood. The man struggling with nature's secrets and her fury was at least aware of his own creatureliness. Those who in medicine or natural science pursued nature's miracles needed not to learn what intellectual reverence meant. Men and women whose highly individual skills, knowledge and experience set an individual value upon themselves could well believe that in God's sight, too, they might count for something.

Of course it is easy to caricature this theme, and point to individual exceptions. It would be stupid to suggest that a man's work alone will make a saint of him. But in general it is true that when work was set against the mystery of life, amid scenes of beauty or the clash of nature's forces, or against the background of ancient and unchanging things, then courage, tradition, spirit, loveliness *mattered* every day. Such conceptions gained familiarity and realism, and found their natural place in worship.

But the modern furnace, factory, mill, mine, production-line, laboratory and railroad do other things to men's souls. Life lived among them may create almost insuperable difficulties for worship, difficulties intellectual, emotional, temperamental and even moral. At the same time, life lived in modern industrial contexts increases the need for worship, which may come to be recognised as the soul's most enduring defence against the worst features of modern life — its ugly connurbations, its destruction of individuality, its innate pride of discovery, its quite false sense of mastery, its vicious competition, its occasonal cruelties.

It may well be that forms of worship suited to one age need to be adjusted to provide maximum help for minds differently conditioned. It probably is true that we moderns have much to relearn of the importance, the values, and the spiritual technique of worship. There is no doubt at all that we have framed for ourselves a manner of life in which all that worship stands for must struggle even to survive. But that worship itself should ever cease, all history, experience, need and moral insight combine to deny.

The command of Jesus, reiterated in the wilderness, sets the call to worship significantly within the deserts of life, where the weary, hungry soul cries out for spiritual refreshment and sustaining truth.

The command of Jesus sets the call to worship sharply within the pressures of temptation, where the beset and fearful soul seeks the holy vision and the heavenly succour that shall save it from its foes.

The command of Jesus sets the call to worship immediately following the dedication to His life work implied in the high hour of His baptism, for without worship man's holiest ideals and noblest projects fail of accomplishment.

And the command of Jesus sets the call to worship, perhaps

most significantly of all, against the shining background of His own proved perfection and immaculate sinlessness. For it is not only when weary with its desert journey, or beset with evil, or striving to attain, that the human soul bows down before its Maker: but when the journey is over, the battle won, the ideal attained, it is still the perfection and the glory of the creature to adore its Creator, and rising in the fullness of a perfected manhood to join with angels and archangels and all the company of heaven in the endless worship of the everlasting God.

23 Behold, Enquire

THE Psalmist's double reason for wanting to dwell in the house of the Lord, "to behold the beauty of the Lord and to enquire in his temple", summarises admirably the twin purposes of all worship. The vision of eternal beauty and the study of eternal truth, lifting up the eyes to the divine loveliness while subjecting the mind to the divine Word, seeing God and seeking His will, together provide a balanced conception of what worship means and form an experience of God which can make every shrine a Bethel, every service rewarding, every Lord's Day a delight.

It is hard to say which of these two purposes is the more necessary. Without either, our worship is poor, our religion itself in peril. To think only of beholding the beauty of the Lord, dwelling upon His gracious ways, His matchless wisdom, His tender patience, His power and glory, is to open the floodgates of the soul to a tide of religious feeling which may, *but may not,* have healthy, useful outlet. Alone, it tends to mere religious sentiment, a profitless emotional aestheticism.

But equally, to think only of getting answers to one's questions, to hurry through the hymn-and-prayer "preliminaries" to see what the sermon has to say, to cross-examine every hymn, analyse the lesson, sift the sermon, impatient to discover new ideas, fresh arguments, novelties of thought, will make worship a barren intellectual exercise which may confirm or provoke our religious opinions but will do little for our souls. We have heads and hearts: God is both wisdom and love: He offers us truth *and* grace. If any worship service lacks either, to that extent its purpose for ourselves has failed.

Whichever be the more important aspect, there can be no doubt which is the more difficult for most people. Many of us are ready enough to argue about religious questions, discuss our disagreements, air our opinions. "To enquire" is a natural and stimulating exercise. But beholding the beauty of the Lord is far removed from disputation: it calls for stillness, reverence, faith, the cessation of argument, the silencing of our insistent — sometimes impudent — questionings, the bowing of the spirit and the upward glance of adoration, love, and thankfulness.

How many of us hear, as we enter the sanctuary, "Take off thy shoes from off thy feet, for the place whereon thou standest is holy ground"; or as we leave can truthfully say, "Mine eyes have seen the King, the Lord of hosts"? Some forms of worship, in striving earnestly for simplicity, sincerity, scripturalness, intimacy, freedom, have forgotten reverence, silence, order, beauty, and the majesty of the Most High. It is easy to become careless in the presence of God, careless about our tongues, our singing, our demeanour; easy, sometimes, to rush in, rush through, rush home, keeping strictly to schedule but without for a moment being inwardly still enough to see the beauty of the Lord or to feel His healing presence.

Yet what is worship if we fail to look away from earth's shadows to the eternal light, from earth's disillusion to the everlasting certainties, from the stain of the world to the holiness of God, from pain and bitterness to the divine tenderness, from earth's falsehoods to the unchanging truth, from man's tragedy to God's throne? Unless we do these things, sitting through a service may be no worship but an exercise in dullness.

But to enquire, with humble and teachable heart, is not so easy as it seems. The Reformers' intention, to set the Bible's pulpit-throne where once the altar stood, turn sacrificing priest into expository preacher, and exalt the Word of God where once the sacramental Host had been uplifted, arose from a true (if sometimes one-sided) insight. Unless worship bring us to the Word of God, and the Word of God to us; unless truth be kindled in the soul; unless the answer of God to prayer, perplexity and doubt be *heard*, worship becomes escapist, unmoral, divorced from reality, an idle hour unrelated to life's serious business.

That is why we need sorely to recover a reverent attitude to preaching. Unfortunately, the true place of the sermon in worship, and of listening as a form of adoration of the Word, is difficult to sustain without seeming to exalt the preacher overmuch. And it must be confessed that sometimes the demand for topicality, for brevity, for interest and even entertainment, and the strong temptation to use the pulpit for the expression of sincere opinions firmly held, rather than for expressing the eternal, *given* Word, have not helped either hearers or speaker to remember what they are about: which is the exposition of the Word of God in the setting of worship under the guidance of the Holy Spirit of truth.

When so many modern folk dare not look up because their heaven is empty, and cannot listen for the illuminating Word because they have not found the Truth, how much more should those who fear the Lord take time and diligent care to behold the beauty of the Lord *and* to enquire in His temple!

24 Leaning on a Gate

IT is a pleasant fancy, and one not altogether idle, that the writer of Ecclesiastes 11 had paused to watch the reapers at their work, and mused, as preachers will, upon the solemn lessons to be learned from things around one. True, he seems not to have decided upon the theme of the sermon, but wanders — again as preachers will — from thoughts of faith and hope to thoughts of generosity and of service to be done. But such things belong together, and the watcher's meditation is not entirely muddled.

One thought is of the great cost of real service (or it may be, of real generosity) and of the consequent need of *faith* to make the investment that either demands. "Cast thy bread upon the waters, for thou shalt find it after many days." The flooding of the fields by swollen rivers in the spring left a rich ooze ready for sowing, and happy was he who could throw his grain plentifully across receding waters.

But there was risk. Among the poor, each grain saved for sowing was a morsel less available for food; and sometimes it seemed like throwing the children's bread upon the tide. Too often in the lean years men went forth "weeping, bearing *precious* seed".

Yet without that risk, that costly sacrifice today for what tomorrow needs, the future will go hungry. We sow in tears: Paul did, Jeremiah did, Jesus did. The sense of wasted effort and unrewarded toil can be hard to bear. But personal success is not the point: the work goes on from generation to generation; "other men laboured, and ye are entered into their labours", and others again will enter into yours. God is not unfair, to forget your labour; and in the final harvest which the angels reap, all faithful sowing finds its fruit. "He shall come again, rejoicing . . . thou shalt find it after many days."

A related thought that crossed the watcher's mind concerns the strange conditions of our service. Often in Palestine agriculture was a chancy business. Small wooden ploughshares and little oxen delayed ploughing until the winter rain had softened the soil — and then "the sluggard will not sow for cold". But the heat of summer was short-lived, and reaping sometimes ran on into autumn storms. To wait for the perfect day was to wait too long. Work must be done in unpropitious times.

Which is certainly true of Christian service, and of Christian charity, for that matter. Wait till you have enough before you give away, and you will never give. Wait for the golden opportunity to serve, and you will die lazy. He that observeth the winds of popular feeling will not sow the seeds of Christian witness; and he that regardeth the cloud of ignorant criticism shall not reap the harvest of Christian achievement. In season, out of season, is the only reasonable motto for God's servants. For in unpropitious times God is often most at work: "as thou knowest not the way of the wind . . . so thou knowest not the works of God, who maketh all."

Through the long hot day the work continues, until as dusk falls the farther edges of the field are being cleared. Neither reapers nor sowers knew an eight-hour day. And watching the last strokes of the flashing knife the Preacher notices how well have grown the last few handfuls of the springtime sowing, thrown by weary hands along the margins of the field. Early and late in the season men must work, morning and evening men must sow and reap. God's work needs continuity, effort sustained as long as strength shall last.

The sudden stir, the hustle and impatience of the young, the high-pressure swing of the mass enterprise are all exciting, and have their place. But character-building is a slow business, and church consolidation, and kingdom-extension, is an all-day job.

Let no man think that sudden in a minute
All is accomplished, and the work is done;
Though with thine earliest dawn thou should'st begin it,
Scarce were it ended with thy setting sun.

There are many excuses why the young should leave all Christian service to the older folk. The days are full, and frequently young help is coldly welcomed. Yet the eagerness, ideas and keenness of the young are often the most precious asset a church possesses. Irresponsible, erratic, sometimes ill-advised, the early zeal of the morning Christian is treasured by the Master: it must be disciplined, directed and — especially — *kept up*.

And in the evening: how often one hears the tragic and humiliating boast, "I used to do . . .". Approach of evening makes the step uncertain, hands weary, hearts more sad, but the work goes on. As shadows gathered around Him, Jesus said, "I must work . . .". So must we. And the service of age is precious,

72

full of experience and skill, grateful, and shrewd and patient. "In the morning sow thy seed, and in the evening withhold not thine hand: for thou knowest not whether shall prosper, either this or that . . . ."

25 Chips, Yokes, and Crosses

AMONG the many transatlantic expressions that have enriched the common English tongue is one whose meaning is elusive and whose origin is apparently in doubt, but which manages nevertheless to be useful and familiar: "the chip upon the shoulder". British authorities agree that it is American. But they vary considerably between relating it, somewhat obscurely, to the carpenter's chips of wood or the mason's chips of stone; to the chips knocked off by rough handling of delicate materials; to the "chips" worn by military officers; to the "chipping at" a person which wears down his patience; and even to the "chipping in" or interference which so often extends the argument it was meant to end.

It seems justifiable to conclude that the origin of the phrase is unknown; and its meaning varies likewise. Quarrelsomeness, a too great readiness to take offence, is suggested by one; a tendency to assert authority beyond official limits is the definition offered by another. Usage, at least in some circles, hardly supports these meanings. A sense of injustice, real or imagined, seems part of the meaning commonly implied: injustice kindling resentment, and tending to get things out of true perspective.

The belief that one has been ill-used, by people, by life, or by God, can quickly develop into a universal grudge, cynical in outlook, bitter in feeling. Such a man comes to have a quarrel against life itself, railing against fate and the unfairness of things. The chip upon the shoulder can then so easily become the rod that breaks his back.

One sure effect of such a sense of being ill-used is to hide from oneself the stiff-necked obstinacy with which we cling to plans or dreams no longer possible and better gracefully re-signed. Another consequence is to hide from our own eyes the unwise decisions, the failures of resolve, the actual faults of character or choice, which produced the situation we resent — and which we are so busily blaming upon others. Yet a third result is to hide from us the constant providence of God: and to obscure His face. For the chip grows, the grievance swells, until we cannot see past it.

"I have been very jealous for the Lord God of hosts: for the children of Israel have forsaken thy covenant, thrown down thine altars, and slain thy prophets with the sword; and I, even I only, am left; and they seek my life to take it away." Elijah is burdened with "chips", until God grants him a humbling insight into the secret working of His power, a new task to do, the assurance that he is not alone as he self-pityingly supposed, and the certainty that the cause would live on. Then, with a fine shrug, the prophet sheds his chips and faith is restored.

Contrast the unencumbered shoulders of the badly misused Joseph. With the accumulated sorrows of long years within his memory, but no bitterness within his heart, he received his brethren with kindness and without reproach. "It was not you that sent me thither, but God . . . to preserve life", he said: the first statement a magnanimous half-truth, the second a magnifi-cent assertion of God's absolute right to use our hard experience to work His gracious will.

In spite of such scriptural examples, the chips will gather, and Christian shoulders are not always clear of them. Life is often unfair: it was so to Christ. Its prizes seem to us to fall to the undeserving. Our load appears unjustly heavy, our duties unusually numerous and unrewarding, our way more difficult to find, more hard to tread, than many another's less conscientious than we!

One spiritual technique for dealing with chips upon the shoulder is to fashion them by faith and prayer into a yoke, and wear it in the spirit of the Master. It may well happen that such an effort will reveal how insubstantial all our grievances really are. But something may remain, perhaps an inherited affliction, a family injustice, responsibility that came unsought and seems unshared, disappointment about something worthily attempted and long prayed for, unavailingly.

Every man must bear his own burden, "carry his own knapsack" as Paul put it, but there is no need to bear it alone. And there is no reason why one's own burden should not be balanced by another's. It is easier that way: one walks the second voluntary mile with lighter step. It needs meekness of heart and lowliness of spirit, as Jesus said, to rid the soul of rebelliousness and wounded pride; but carried Jesus' way the yoke is easy and the burden light.

The other spiritual technique for dealing with chips upon the shoulder is to see them transfigured by the light of Calvary into the fashion of a cross. Not every complaint and burden of the heart may be so transformed. Some, enormous in our eyes, are really too trivial. Others are too selfish, and yet others are our own fault, and wholly unrelated to any faithfulness to Christ. But where the burden is His appointment for us, where the heaviness of heart is truly the price we are paying for loyalty to His will, then the things that oppress are indeed part of Calvary. When that is clearly seen, complaint is churlish, resentment totally out of place. To share His cross and "complete what is lacking in Christ's afflictions for the sake of his body, the church", is the highest privilege any Christian can know, and in the end the deepest peace.

26 Too Old at Forty!

ONE comparatively recent and universal trend within the Christian Church has been the astonishing emphasis laid upon youth. It is hard to believe that for the first nineteen of its twenty centuries the Christian society possessed no Youth Departments, but expected young people to share spiritual things with their elders, as they shared natural things, in the unity of the family.

Concentration of special methods upon the winning of young hearts has doubtless much to commend it, but no one will imagine that it has been all gain. Certainly it has given youth an exaggerated idea of its own importance, and especially of its value: few indeed of our churches would survive if they depended upon the under-twenty-fives! Certainly, too, the segregation of young people's societies from the general fellowship of the Church can mean the progressive deterioration of standards in youth work — youth after all has so little to share with youth. And certainly, again, the total life of the whole Church has suffered by the separation of the ages, the old becoming prematurely aged, and the young remaining too long adolescent, for want of contact with each other.

But perhaps the saddest, and even the most serious, loss has been the decline in belief in the possibility of new spiritual experience when youth has passed. We are in danger of thinking that if men are not Christians by thirty years of age, they never will be; that after forty there is little left to discover of Christian life except a new appreciation of the Christian hope; that in fact God is only really interested in the under-twenties!

There is, of course, a modicum of truth in this: at any rate, it is true that difficulties multiply within the thirties. Responsibilities increase, life becomes intensely busy, mentally and morally the soul gets into ruts; there are many things to regret, and some it is hard to forgive onself; and strangest of all, a new spiritual shyness develops which hates to "lose face" by becoming religious. Middle age has its spiritual doldrums: Bunyan called it the enchanted ground, where the air tended to make one drowsy!

But did not Jesus warn against the preoccupations that like thorns would choke the seed of truth? The question is whether the ruts are comfortable, whether the habits are satisfactory, whether the regrets must simply be left to turn to bitterness. Christian life is not a leisure-time pursuit for those with nothing else to do; nor is it a hobby, or an enthusiasm, for the immature. There is every possibility of untold discovery

76

and enrichment when maturer hearts, with reasoned faith and disciplined will and *deeper* emotions, seek God.

Besides, the older Christian often counts for more. The wider influence, the deeper experience, the broader knowledge, the fuller personality can offer Christ a stronger, steadier, wiser service and sometimes a deeper consecration. The Church needs such: and whether they realise it or not, the young need such. "The middle-aged," says George Eliot, "who have lived through their strongest emotions, but are yet in the time when memory is still half-passionate, should be a sort of natural priesthood, whom life has disciplined and consecrated to be the refuge and the rescue of early stumblers and victims of despair".

Many a pastoral selection committee might pin that on their agenda! Counsellors, friends, and guides of youth must be themselves beyond the follies, confusions, dogmatisms and doubts that comprise youth's problem. Churches electing youth leaders and deacons and workers of all kinds should not forget the special contribution a man or woman can make when speech is just a little more thoughtful, reactions a little slower and wiser, fanaticisms somewhat more balanced, and appreciation of the values of tradition and experience is just a little more keen, than once it was. To be young, and to be Christian, is glorious: but it is not everything.

One wonders how old Luke was when the book of Acts was written. In chapter 2 old men dream dreams. In 3 and 4, "the man was above forty years old on whom this miracle was shewed". In chapter 10, Cornelius, and in 16, the jailor begin life again in middle age. Paul was about forty when his life-work began. Luther, Wesley, Carey were in their third decade at the turning points in life; and so also were Elizabeth Fry and Florence Nightingale. Schweitzer was thirty-eight when Africa called.

The Christ who can satisfy the turbulent demands of youth, and comfort and carry the weakness of age, is not baffled by the problems, nor unmoved by the wistfulness, of middle age. No one can outgrow the richness of His teaching, the challenge of His example, the thrill of His fellowship, the endless possibilities of exploring new ways to serve His cause. The Lord can revive His work in the midst of the years, and in the midway stretch can make Himself known. Luke is right: many a man is well above forty on whom miracles of grace are shown.

27 A Good Man

BUNYAN'S varied gallery of portraits contains none more attractive than Mr. Greatheart, a kindly, understanding, "encouraging person", appointed for the rescue of the imperilled, the counselling of the perplexed, the shepherding of the wayward, and the refreshment of the weary who travel on the King's highway. For that endearing character the New Testament model was undoubtedly Barnabas, companion of apostles and servant of the Church, "a good man, full of the Holy Ghost, and of faith".

A good man: the only man so described in the whole of scripture. We do well to honour him, if only because he took so little care to honour himself. And because we may discern in him the lineaments of one after Christ's own heart.

Luke introduces Barnabas to us first as a man of generous heart and hand, who on coming to Christ brought freely to the common Christian purse the proceeds of land and property, to lay all at the apostles' feet. Thus early did he manifest that selfless and wholehearted love which made him invaluable in Christ's service. A man whose pocket and fortunes are saved is saved indeed.

To the generous hand was matched a generous mind. News reached Jerusalem of the conversion of the most skilful opponent of the harassed Church, but not all could believe it true. When in due time there arrived at the capital the ardent and eager convert, there were not wanting those who suspected some trick and were for holding Paul at arm's length, "in case". Barnabas must have seen reason in such caution, but he saw other things as well — the greatness of Christ's power and the depth of His mercy, and (can we doubt it?) the anguish and disappointment in the heart of Paul. So Barnabas went forth to offer the right hand of fellowship and bringing him to the apostles stood surety for his good faith. The significance of such an action cannot be exaggerated. A similar friendship and magnanimity within the Church would have saved for her fellowship many a "lost" new convert.

Scarcely surprising, then, that Barnabas was the man sent to investigate strange new happenings at Antioch, where a wholly Gentile Church had been founded without apostolic initiative, leadership, or authority. From subsequent events we know that many things at Antioch needed wise and continued attention in the new Church's life. But beneath the novelty, strangeness and immaturity, Barnabas "saw the grace of God, and was glad". It is open to debate whether Barnabas' decision reflects most credit upon himself or upon those who selected so gracious and so fitting a delegate. What is beyond question is that every raw, new Christian cause, on the mission field or at home, un-organised, exuberant, inexperienced, unbalanced, needs just the sympathetic insight and far-seeing faith that Barnabas displayed.

Coming with full authority of the Church at Jerusalem, Barnabas might justly have appointed himself leader and re-former of the Church at Antioch. But such was not his way. He knows that away at Tarsus a brilliant young Christian Pharisee has been slowly prepared of the Lord for such a task, and he introduces Paul to Antioch. So by the grace of Barnabas the younger man is given his first great opportunity, so fraught with immeasurable promise for the years to come.

Nor is that all. For this good man, who first brought Paul within the apostolic fellowship and now first opens for him the door of official service, stayed on at Antioch a whole year, playing "second fiddle" to the younger man, counselling, advising, supporting with authority, doubtless sometimes also restraining, without jealousy, rancour or mistrust. In this way was forged, by the selflessness of Barnabas, a comradeship in Christ which was to carry these two far in the work of the gospel.

But still the story is not done. He who befriended Paul in his rejection later befriended Mark when Paul himself was stern. For Mark had deserted from the first missionary journey; and desertion, cowardice or indecision were not qualities with which Paul found it easy to be patient. When therefore Mark would join the second journey, Paul declines his help.

But Barnabas the generous and gentle reads another eager, disappointed heart, willing to retrace its erring steps if given the chance; and Barnabas stands by Mark, even to the sacrifice of Paul's companionship. So Barnabas and Mark went off to Cyprus, and once more young and old together did great things for Christ — thanks to Barnabas.

The later Church has owed more than any man can measure to the genius of Paul as thinker, evangelist, correspondent, protagonist and saint; and it has owed scarcely less to Mark, whose story of Jesus was the pioneer and the basis of all accounts of our Lord. But, under God, the Church owes Paul and Mark to Barnabas: and we do not always remember that debt. It was Alexander Maclaren who said that if he must choose he preferred the grace of Barnabas to the genius of Paul, and none with pastoral experience will doubt that valuation.

The Greatheart of the New Testament was a *good* man. In such generosity of hand and heart, of mind and friendship, of strength and loyalty and selflessness, Christian goodness still consists.

28 Good Men Gone Wrong

JUDAISM was fortunate to possess, in the years of sorest trial, a group of earnest and tenacious men utterly devoted to the Jewish faith. These "saints", or "pious ones", formed a kind of spiritual freemasonry, alongside and overlapping the official groups; and from their diligence and zeal the hard-pressed Jewish state drew such faith and fervent strength as it possessed.

One meaning of their name, the "separatists", suggests a parallel with the Puritans, and the likeness is not wholly accidental. They, too, had proved their willingness to contend for religious principle upon the battlefield. First Greeks and then Romans sought to impose by force their alien ways and laws, language and religion, upon the Jewish people: but there were men prepared to fight and suffer, starve and die for freedom to obey the laws of God. Through the long Maccabean struggle the "godly ones" (to use yet another nickname) resisted stoutly until spiritual freedom was assured. Then, when others would continue the fight for merely political ends, they quietly withdrew, uninterested.

But their struggle did not end with fighting. It was needful to resist encroachment by every possible means: pagan books and tongues, dress, games, coins and forms of culture were all rigorously rejected. In reply, everything Jewish was emphasised to the point of exaggeration — dress, customs, laws, food, table manners, festivals, names, the Sabbath, circumcision. The "hallowed ones" kept clear of every appearance of heathenism, refusing to walk in the counsel of the ungodly, to stand in the way of sinners, or to sit in the seat of the scornful even of their own race.

Behind this Puritan staunchness lay an evangelical passion. Their stand was costly, and involved opprobrium, but they stood together. Drawn mainly from the wealthier classes, they propagated their standards via the synagogue throughout the Mediterranean world. They tithed their wealth with scrupulous care, and sacrificed advancement whenever compromise was implied. Their family morality was the envy of the pagan. God, the law, and the hope of the Messiah formed their creed; prayer, fasting, almsgiving was their code; washings, festival-observance and memorising scripture was their discipline; teaching the children, preaching in the synagogues, converting the heathen, maintaining the law was their consecrated task.

More spiritual than the Sadducees, they understood and emphasised the transcendence of God. They believed in angels, spirits, and the resurrection; they lived in daily expectation of Messiah; they accepted the whole unseen world with solemn earnestness. United, zealous, generous, dogmatic, patriotic,

Puritan, missionary-hearted, Bible-loving, they well deserve the title Evangelicals of Judaism.

And yet their name became a byword and reproach — "Thou Pharisee!" Sharing with the scribes the religion based on law, they, too, made piety a burden, judged chiefly by external standards, and often emphasised the unimportant ritual detail to the neglect of greater moral duties. They were probably even more prone than the scribes to trim their conduct to the literal words of scripture, even when the spirit and effect of what they did was wrong.

The freer attitude of Jesus toward the tradition of the elders outraged their sense of right, and His friendship with the outcast and the heathen denied their central principle of separation. Nor could they, with their faith in an all-sufficient bygone revelation, find room for the immediate authority of Jesus, as One speaking from God.

The Master, for His part, did not spare the Pharisees. He sharply criticised their over-emphasis on ritual washings instead of purity of heart, their contemptuous attitude to common folk, their ostentation, and their social and religious pride. He castigated severely the moral wrongs committed under shelter of the letter of the law. Their self-assurance, confident that their own good works sufficed before God, Jesus declared to be gross self-deception; while much that they prized as setting a good example He dismissed as mere play-acting, adequately rewarded by their reputation with the "gallery".

Yet these men were Puritans and Evangelicals after the forms and within the terms of their historic faith. Not Judaism alone, but the Christian Church also owes much to Pharisaism — Christianity has special cause to be grateful for the preparation for the gospel laid by these men in the synagogues and in men like Paul. So fine a line is drawn between the zeal, conviction, ardour that can accomplish much for God, and the passion, bigotry, blindness and ruthlessness that crucified the Christ!

Where precisely does a healthy puritanism slip over the boundaries of truth into what is merely puritannical? How does zeal for faithful witness and a genuinely good example degenerate into religious exhibitionism? At what point does true concern to keep oneself unspotted from the world become an exclusive isolationism and spiritual snobbery? Where does minding one's own spiritual business become simple selfishness?

Walking circumspectly toward them that are without so easily becomes just toadying for good opinions; pride in one's church, one's work, one's spiritual tradition slips so readily into pride of one's own achievement, and so into self-righteousness. And a well-meant faithfulnes to what is written, or has been long believed, can make the soul insensitive to new moral challenges and the leading of the Spirit.

The tragic story of the Pharisees reads us a lesson as solemn as any in the New Testament: how easily earnest good men go wrong. But where exactly our safeguard lies is far from clear.

Would it be simply in *humility?*

29 Division and Disaster

JESUS dismissed as patent nonsense the charge brought against Himself that He was in league with Satan in casting out demons. The accusation is self-refuting. Any power divided against itself destroys itself; the more strong and efficient it is, the more certainly and efficiently does it do it. The devil, Jesus suggests, understood that well enough, if the scribes did not. It is a simple, and indeed obvious, truth — even if the modern Church has not yet entirely measured its significance. It is not merely that division brings disaster: division *is* disaster.

That is sadly true within the state. "Every kingdom divided against itself is brought to desolation." The Jews knew it in Maccabean days, and were to learn it again with tragic finality in A.D. 70. Rome, too, was to learn it in her turn. Twenty years of French history tell the same tale. It can happen in any state, and the cost of internal strife is exceedingly high. No public issue is squarely faced, few national problems resolutely tackled, every programme of action fashioned by compromise, or by reaction, between rival parties.

Whenever sectional interests reduce public policy to hard bargaining on claim and counter-claim, the welfare of all is likely to be sacrificed to the ambition of the best organised or most vocal group. Legitimate differences of opinion, fostered in suspicion, harden into diversities of aim; and the lack of any common loyalty to the whole, any agreed and final basis of morality, any uniting spiritual vision, makes it inevitable that unless new wisdom comes the highest interests of the state must perish.

The danger lies not so much in the triumph of this or that idea, but in the inability, or unwillingness, to find a common ground of co-operation and discipline. The division is itself destructive.

The principle is no less true within the home. "Every house divided against itself shall not stand." A home united within itself no external circumstances can break: trouble, illness, poverty, adversity may even serve to deepen loyalty and nourish love. But a home disunited no external circumstances can bind together: money, social position, family disapproval, self-interest cannot effect more than a grim façade of unity held together by pride.

It would be hard to say which breach of loyalty within the home of Isaac and Rebekah was the most tragic. That between the brothers, Jacob and Esau, was the origin of agelong enmity. That between the sons and the parents, Esau defying and Jacob deceiving the aged Isaac, was perhaps the most graceless. But that between Rebekah and Isaac — over Jacob — was the origin of all else, and the near-ruin of Jacob. The disunity of father and mother is the end of all parental authority, in every age; and jealousy for the child's affection is the root cause of indiscipline in countless homes.

Differences of educational and social environment make the gulf between the generations especially troublesome in our age, but they can be made to enrich family life where affection is retained. Marriage itself, as we see with increasing clearness, cannot survive on mutual attraction alone: it needs the additional bond of a shared loyalty to supreme things that the passage of time cannot wither. Howsoever one studies the "problem family", the truth remains insistent that only a deliberately enthroned unity of heart and spirit, jealously preserved, can avert disaster from home and youth.

And the word holds true also for the Church. Possibly Matthew meant us to remember this when he added in the same context, about discipleship, the saying, "He that is not with me is against me". To be ardently for Christ is to have a right to the sympathy and loyalty of all others who are for Him. The sharper the divisions of the Church from the world, the more imperative becomes the unity of Christians among themselves.

The divided Church is powerless, joyless, prayerless, useless. That one party in any division will be sure that it is more faithful to Christ, more loyal to truth, more "spiritual", prayerful, evangelical, makes not the slightest difference. The division is the disaster. The tragedy is that those who, with high-sounding arguments, insist upon their own way "lest the Church be doomed", cannot see that the Church they are dividing is already doomed — and by themselves.

The accusation arose because Jesus had healed a distracted soul. The individual life is not exempt from the same plain peril. The divided mind reaches no understanding; the divided heart finds no rest; the divided soul knows no security; the divided life possesses no influence. Whether the division lies in deliberate hypocrisy, in the conflict of flesh with spirit, or in mental uncertainty about committing oneself to Christ, the double-minded man is always unstable — and unsafe.

On every level Jesus offers Himself as the reconciling Lord, who can bind together the factions of society, the members of the home, the individuals within a church, the elements of personality. He offers a love, a kingdom, a vocation that integrate life's disruptive forces under His unifying mastery. Dividedness always spells disaster, but the testimony of the past is sure: "Christ Jesus maketh . . . whole."

30 Misdirected Invitation

So rarely did Jesus refuse requests for help that such refusal, when it came, must be instructive — especially for hearts to whom the failure of prayer is the most painful of all spiritual disciplines.

A quarrel about family property and the right division of inheritance was brought to Jesus for judgement. Doubtless the usual processes of law had failed to satisfy, or had been avoided as too uncertain or too costly. But Jesus is a prophet, speaking up for justice and the common people: to Him the aggrieved brother turns to bring pressure upon the selfish heir. But Jesus declines to intervene. For one thing, He is neither judge nor arbitrator, as the appellant himself would certainly point out if the decision were given against him. And where authority is questioned, arbitration is mere meddling.

To refusal is added warning: "Beware of covetousness"; and the warning draws attention to two serious and all-too-common shortcomings in the plea for help.

One blunder lay in asking Jesus to pronounce upon the matter and telling Him what to say. "Lord, speak to my brother that he divide the inheritance with me." But to divide or not divide was the precise matter supposedly submitted to Christ's judgement; this is the point at issue. The man desires no impartial verdict, he wants only support for his case. And to that attitude of mind the Master has nothing to say.

We frequently seek guidance with our minds made up, and receiving no answer feel forsaken and unblessed. Scripture seems stale, and irrelevant, prayer unsatisfying, sermons "out of touch", friendly counsel lacking in understanding, because we wish only confirmation of our own opinions, new reasons for decisions already reached. So Herod found Jesus disappointing, and Jesus stood in resolute silence before him, because Herod's mind was long made up, his resistance to the kingdom now unalterable. So Pilate, too, was exasperated by Jesus' refusal to argue or plead. Sufficient explanation being given, sufficient information for a just verdict, Jesus says no more: responsibility is clearly upon Pilate.

On such occasions God is always silent. Prayer is no substitute for obedience, and the request for guidance when we are resolved what we shall do is mere idling with conscience and with God. The answering word is given to those who pray: "Lord, speak . . . and say just what You will."

A yet greater mistake lay in the form of the request: "Lord, speak to my brother . . . ." We are not really surprised at Christ's reply, "Never mind your brother — you beware of covetousness!" We are always sure the fault lies with the other man. He it is who should apologise, who needs a more Christian attitude, a better spirit. It is the Russians, the outsiders, the other denomination, the disagreeable folk who disagree with us, who need the Master's word! And all the time He waits to speak with *us*.

"Lord, speak to my brother!" Sometimes it represents evasion of too personal a truth. We fit the sermon on to others' shoulders, applaud the "searching" references to others' sins, take refuge in the wide world's needs against too sharp awareness of our own. "John Ware of Cambridge," wrote Longfellow, "preached a good sermon; I applied it to myself". That is why it seemed so good. Listening by proxy is an effective barricade against the truth, but very costly when Jesus waits to speak with us.

"Lord, speak to my brother!" Occasionally it represents a defence-mechanism against too uncomfortable a judgement. David's moral indignation against deceit and covetousness inspired a noble eloquence — until cut short by Nathan's stern "Thou art the man!" Felix felt it necessary to adjourn the hearing when it proved to be himself and not the apostle who was under cross-examination. We all "compound for sins we are inclined to, by damning those we have no mind to", forgetting the dreadful warning that with what judgement we judge, we shall be judged.

"Lord, speak to my brother!" It can be made a shield against too challenging a duty. Convicted, challenged, warned, we take refuge in the fact that others feel no such qualms of conscience as now trouble us. Let God speak to others first, then if they hear so will I! To which, if Jesus speaks at all, He will but say, as He said to Peter's question about John —

"Lord, what will this man do?" — the sharp, "What is that to thee? follow thou me". The self-justifying "What about him?" has no place on Christian lips.

And every minister has met the plea disguised as an earnest zeal for evangelistic enterprise or a consuming social concern. "Preach the gospel," he is told, "that wins outsiders". And looking around his congregation the preacher knows within his heart that the only certain thing about outsiders is that they are outside. "Preach to the absent, preach to society, preach about the sins of our age. . . . What about a strong sermon on Africa, or China, or Moscow? What about a straight talk to the beatniks? Speak boldly, speak plain, but speak to my erring, anonymous, absent brother — for I'm all right!"

We all do it at some time and in some fashion. But we rarely get reply until, in altered tones, we truly pray, Lord, speak to *me* . . . .

31 Surrounded

M OSES' final benediction upon Israel, as recorded in Deuteronomy, is one of the grandest, and most comprehensive, promises in all scripture, but it is to be feared that not all its meaning is familiar. We lose much of its assurance by remembering, oddly, only its final words — about the everlasting arms that are underneath. We lose something more, perhaps, because the promise is couched in the language of poetry, and the highly imaginative poetry of the ancient East at that. But the meaning is precise, and clear, and deeply reassuring.

"There is none like unto the God of Jeshurun" — the upright ones — "who rideth upon the heaven to thy help, and in his excellency upon the sky . . . ." Moses is thinking of the manifold dangers that threaten man's welfare from above: the storms and thunderclouds, the blazing, scorching sun and the fateful moon, the swift stroke of the lightning and the murderous hail — all those higher, untameable powers of nature that sometimes wreak havoc upon man's puny defencelessness. For us the essential significance of such fears is immensely magnified by our sense of a measureless universe whose distances and imprisoned forces terrify even as they baffle the human imagination.

Even more acutely than the ancient Hebrews, we feel our naked creatureliness, vulnerable and mortal, set in the midst of powers we can neither understand nor control. Earthquake, typhoon, flood and nuclear explosion evoke in us the same feeling of helpless littleness that seized the early Israelite as the mountain smoked, or the thunderstorm roared through the narrow gorges, or the baneful moon with unwinking stare drew the remaining wits from the weak-minded.

But God is above us: He rideth upon the heaven to our help; His majesty is known within the skies. He maketh the clouds His chariots, His faithfulness reaches unto the storm-wrack and He rideth upon the tempest. The stars tell the greatness of His power, the heavens declare His glory, and He is thy shade upon thy right hand that the sun may not smite thee by day nor the moon by night. All of which means, in plain prose and the experience of faith, that the great God of Nature is on our side, and we are guarded and guided by the God who is above us.

But there are things that threaten the upright soul not only from above but from round about. There are temptations that press in from the evil world, conflicts waged by the soul against the pressure of society, the down-drag of environment and the hindrance of circumstance. There is the burden of a man's duty, the weight of his afflictions, and all that arises from a man's surroundings and situation to threaten the peace, the poise, or the purity of his soul.

We are probably far more keenly aware of such environmental dangers to the good life than were those for whom Moses spoke: but the promise to Israel is matched also to this peril — "the eternal God is thy refuge . . .". The idea is of a place of safe retreat, a strong tower wherein the soul may hide from enemies too powerful to face. He that dwelleth in the secret place of the Most High shall abide — shall continue in safety

— in the shadow of the Almighty. As the mother hen gathers her chicks beneath her breast at the first sign of danger, so God shall cover thee with His feathers, and under His wings shalt thou trust. Thou shalt not be afraid:

> *The storm may roar without me,*
> *My heart may low be laid,*
> *But God is round about me*
> *And can I be dismayed?*

Can I indeed, when the eternal God is my Refuge?

And so Moses comes to the God who is beneath us: "underneath are the everlasting arms." This thought is much less familiar, but how needful! We may rightly read our way by the stars above, bravely face out the storms around, but we shall never arrive safely if we ignore the rocks, the quicksands, the shoals and currents and mud that lurk beneath.

There is a dangerous underneath in social life, in the slums and vice and crime that deface our brave new world. There is a dangerous underneath in private life, that dim world of the subconscious where half-forgotten things, half-forgiven things, half-conquered things, half-repented sins, half-banished fears, half-stifled desires lie repressed and hoarded in the dark underworld of the mind ready to cause endless nervous, moral and spiritual troubles. And there is an underneath of experience, when the soul is cast down by sorrow, weighed down by trouble, borne down by opposition, or sinks down in sin. How very often the real dangers to the soul come, not from above or around but from beneath, and how well therefore the great promise moves on from the God who is above and around us to the God who is beneath — for "underneath the underneath" is the love, and strength, the grip, the embrace, of the everlasting arms.

Underneath our direst need: for when we are beyond our strength and at the end of our tether and out of our depth, the Lord will take us up. When we have fallen through storey after storey of our strength and pride and hope, and sit on the brink of despair, then for the upright in heart the everlasting arms close in and hold.

90

Man, what is this, and why art thou despairing?
God shall forgive thee all but thy despair.

Underneath our desperate weakness: for when in the struggles for truth and right the heart sinks down with the sense of its own frailty and failure, then the mighty arm and the out-stretched hand of the Lord of hosts supports the fainthearted. Paul found it so, being troubled but not distressed, perplexed but not in despair, persecuted but not forsaken, cast down but not destroyed. God has never let down the weakest soul that trusted in Him. We may be beaten to our knees, but there — there especially, we shall find that still underneath are the everlasting arms.

Underneath our deepest sorrow: for when the soul plunges into the gloom of the valley of the shadow, and sinks alone in the darkness of death, there, too, are the arms of God to support, and comfort, and uphold. His arms are *everlasting* arms; the souls of the righteous are in the hand of God; and nothing shall separate us from the love of God, neither life nor death, things present nor things to come. And in God's outstretched hand is the gift of immortality.

Underneath our darkest sin, too: for the Lord's hand is not shortened, that it cannot save. We fall precipitously into the pit of sin, we sink down low in thought and desire and act, we plunge in shame, but we cannot fall beyond the reach of the everlasting arms. The first touch of penitence, the first prayer of contrition, the first feeble cry for cleansing, finds the love of God close in and hold with unrelaxing grip. None can fall so low that the arms of God are not still beneath him — and his sin.

At Calvary Jesus proved it true. Standing in our direst need, sharing our desperate weakness, tasting our deepest sorrow, dying for our darkest sin, He in the darkness and agony of that lonely hour sank deeper and deeper into the pit of sorrow, suffering and shame until from His lips was wrung the anguished cry, "My God, my God, why hast thou forsaken me?" And then He found the everlasting arms close in and hold, and in utter peace He sighed, "Father, into thy hands . . .".

Above, around, beneath, we are encircled with the love and care of God: *why* should we be so fearful?

32 The Cupboard Was Bare

IT was a simple point that Jesus wished to illustrate: that if a thing was really worth the praying for, it was well to keep on asking till you got it. Ask, seek, and even knock, for when prayer's sincerity has been proved by importunity it is likelier to prevail. This is clear, once said. Why then did Jesus tell the story as He did? Who is this inconsiderate friend A who makes his journey unannounced relying on friend B, who finds his larder empty and must go borrowing of friend C?

This at least is plain: the occasion that sends the poor man scurrying through the darkened streets at midnight, rapping on a neighbour's door, swallowing his pride and confessing the inhospitable bareness of his cupboards, is not his own hunger, nor a spell of overdue spring-cleaning. It is the simple fact that someone has come to him for help and found him wanting.

Nothing reveals spiritual poverty like the sudden need of others. We feel all right, think ourselves in reasonable spiritual health, compare ourselves with others without shame, and look with true concern on the unsaved. Then someone seeks a blessing at our door — and suddenly we know our poverty. The quality of every Christian life is measured by its overflow; not by how long you have been a Christian, or how you have enjoyed it, or what great preachers you have heard or privileges you have known, but by what you have been able to share with hearts in need.

Who is this friend who comes so inconveniently to expose our spiritual want? Sometimes it is our children, growing up beset with questions, temptations, problems, doubts, in a world that we ourselves can barely understand. They lie heavy on our hearts; and the more we seek to guide them, counsel, teach and shield them, so the more we realise our own shortcomings — how shallow our faith, how incomplete our grasp of fundamental things, how fitful our own loyalty to Christ. We find, so often, that we have not the resources to help our children; we cannot pass on what we do not possess.

Sometimes it is a neighbour, whom we never suspected of

spiritual interest or need. Stricken with illness, broken with grief, wounded by another's wrong, she turns quite unexpectedly to us for comfort, "knowing we are churchgoing folk". But it is midnight with us, and the shelves are empty: we cannot share what we have long since ceased to enjoy.

Sometimes it is the young folk rising in the Church, making their own first faltering steps of faith, and their so noisy blunders; dedicating young and eager hearts with troublesome enthusiasm to the work of Christ. They are discovering, with dismay, how much of snobbishness and coolness, criticism and unconcern directs our ways, and too often they go off to some more "lively" church and leave us in our peaceful groove. Another stranger has called at the inconvenient hour and rudely exposed our want of spiritual power. We cannot communicate what has died out of our common life.

Or sometimes, it may be, a soul has found Christ overnight, in some campaign, or private interview. Eagerly, alert, he turns back to us for nourishment, for fellowship and understanding, and an outlet for his energies. But the ordinary routine of church life lacks that "something" the campaign possessed. Now and again perhaps a soul might seek us out with breaking heart and contrite spirit, heavy with a load of sin, and plead with us to tell him what he must do to be saved. How many earnest and sincere church folk have the answer to that plea — honestly — in their cupboard?

This surely is in the story Jesus told: the emergency of others brings home to us our need. The condemnation of a Christian life on bare subsistence level — one service on Sunday and prayer when you are ill — is that it pays no dividend, possesses no overflow, must turn away the hungry, for it has no grace to spare.

Or else it must find some other friend with bread enough and to spare, and seek at once and urgently a fresh supply. The stale crusts of an almost forgotten spiritual experience, or a church's long-standing, now fading, evangelical tradition, will not do. The spiritual grace that overflows the individual soul, and fills with fragrance and with power the fellowship of the Church, must be kept fresh. We need to be ever seeking, asking, pleading, that our stock shall be renewed if the hungry are not to be turned unhelped and desperate from our door.

"And he will give . . . as much as he needeth." Let us have no doubt of that. The reluctant friend in the parable, not short of provisions but of patience, not troubled about the bread but at the bother, even he will rise from bed, disturbing the children, unlock the door and lade his neighbour — if he keep on asking urgently enough. How much more God, the unreluctant Friend, more ready to give than we to ask, will give enough and to spare when we plead the needs of others. For all spiritual overflow is borrowed; our sufficiency is of God, and our poverty is entirely our own fault. The cupboard is bare through want of prayer. Just that.

33 If Thou Knewest!

CONFRONTING Jesus across the well-head at Sychar, the woman of Samaria stood all unconsciously on the threshold of the greatest experience possible to human hearts. She was face to face with Christ, knowing Him, talking with Him, ready to pour out to Him her soul and her story. And He has spoken to her, has offered to her parched soul the water of life, has already begun to lead towards the great discovery. Sinner and Saviour, bitter need and abundant supply, a stained and sordid life and the redeeming power and love to cleanse it thoroughly, are here brought together, within reach. Anything good and glorious can happen.

But the transforming miracle halts. The conversation wanders. Her salvation waits, and her apprehension remains elementary. For a time it appears she might linger where so many seem to linger: within reach of Christ, confronted with His claim and invitation, moved toward Him, yet somehow still but on the threshold. She is much nearer to Christ, and to salvation, than many who have never consented to the face-to-face encounter: but she is not near enough. What, then, is wanting?

The answer of Jesus is somewhat surprising: She does not *know* enough. "If thou knewest . . .". One inescapable condition of fullness of Christian experience is fullness of spiritual understanding, an instructed mind, a soul nourished on the truth of God.

Ignorance in Christians is blamed for many things by the New Testament writers. It underlies the immaturity and quarrelsomeness of believers at Corinth. It leaves the Ephesian converts at the mercy of every wind of doctrine and the cunning of deceitful men. It causes the long-standing Hebrew Christians to be ill-qualified to teach others when such service might justly be expected of them.

Immature, unstable, useless — it is a sharp indictment of spiritual ignorance. But Jesus implies more: that lack of knowledge stunts experience. All would acknowledge this at the beginning of Christian life. "Faith cometh by hearing, and hearing by the word of God. But how shall they believe in him of whom they have not heard?" But the same is true equally of later stages and deeper experiences of God.

When Paul discovered certain disciples at Ephesus whose level of experience and enjoyment prompted the question, "Did you receive the Holy Ghost when you believed?" he received the answer, "We have not so much as heard if there be any Holy Ghost." That is a reply to be pondered by all who preach, or teach, and by all who learn — or resist instruction. Experience waits upon knowledge: and we cannot enter into blessing, or the deeper things of God, if we have not so much as heard that God has them in store for us.

So Paul's prayer for the Ephesians is that they might be enriched in all wisdom and knowledge, given the Spirit of wisdom and revelation in the knowledge of Christ, the eyes of their understanding being enlightened that they might know what is the hope of their calling, what the riches of the glory of their inheritance, and what the exceeding greatness of God's power. Because unless they know these things, they will never experience them. It is true that knowledge by itself is not religion, and that knowledge prized for its own sake is barren and conceited. But knowledge as the guide to experiment, exploration and experience is indispensable, if we are to follow on to know the Lord.

The immediate effect of knowledge is awakened desire, a stimulated faith, a wider expectation, a more eager prayer. "If thou knewest . . . thou wouldest have asked!" Prayer, too, is circumscribed by ignorance, and deepened and broadened by spiritual instruction.

Listening to Jesus expounding the Bread of life, the hearers burst out spontaneously, "Lord, evermore give us this bread". So the woman at Sychar, beginning to understand, cries, "Sir, give me this water, that I thirst not . . .". Confronted with the power of Jesus, and understanding better His gracious promise, a man breaks out: "Lord, I believe: help thou mine unbelief." The swift reaction to newly revealed possibilities of greater blessing is always "Lord, do *that* for me!"

We drift along in a dull routine of uninspired Christian life, maintaining just enough prayer to keep us afloat: then something reveals to us our shallowness — news of revival and growth elsewhere, or contact with a radiant Christian soul, or an illuminating passage of the Word. And out of the new vision of what God wants, and wills, to do for us is born the prayer that He will do, and give, and be, all He intends, and makes us willing for all He asks. Such knowledge, kindling into desire and pouring forth in prayer, is the way to revival — and the only way.

"If thou knewest . . . thou wouldest have asked . . . and he would have given . . . ." The final emphasis must be there, on the free giving of God. Not all our knowledge, certainly not all our praying, will bring the fullness of grace and power we desire: first and last and to the end it is the gift of God. The great danger of a high valuation of spiritual knowledge is intellectual pride; the peril of emphasising the importance of prayer lies in the ease with which we come to think that our praying, and not God's giving, explains the blessing! We tend to think that by our spiritual wisdom or our importunity in prayer we are "compelling" the blessing, constraining the Lord to do as we wish.

All such thoughts are fallen from *grace* to works, to self-righteousness, to Pharisaism. Knowledge and prayer are but preparation: the gift is God's. But He wills to give, ever more fully, ever more wonderfully. He wants us to go forward in experience, in power, and in enjoyment. But the pattern of progress cannot be by-passed: If thou knewest . . . thou wouldest have asked . . . and He would have given.

34 Purposeful Providence

THE first thing always to be said about Paul's great declaration that all things work together for good to them that love God is that it is the considered utterance of a man with both eyes wide open to the realities of life. This is no comfortable self-assurance bred of cushioned armchairs in a secure and cosy study, no exalted theory of providence debated at leisure in some secluded cloister. It is a deep and reasoned conviction hammered out in a long and arduous life by one who had travelled most of the known world, had suffered far more than most men, and had done battle daily with the ignorance and sin of humanity.

The famous saying occurs in a passage immediately concerned with infirmities and groanings, tribulation, distress, persecution, famine, nakedness, peril and the sword, with things present that oppress and things to come that threaten, with all the vicissitudes of life and all the darkness of death. With these things on the surface of his mind Paul wrote that all things work together for good. And if the saying be set in the wider context of the apostle's experience, it must be remembered that Paul had been treated with suspicion by men to whom he had looked for loyalty; he had been let down by unworthy colleagues; he had tasted poverty and the hardest manual toil; he had been roughly handled in most of the greater towns and cities of the Roman empire; he had been beaten, plotted against, stoned, shipwrecked; he had fought with physical infirmity throughout a most active career; he had been wrongfully arrested, unfairly imprisoned, unjustly tried, and ever over his life hung the threat of martyrdom. This is the man who could write, deliberately and with full honesty, "We know that all things work together for good . . .".

We certainly cannot dismiss the saying, therefore, as the airy optimism of a man for whom life had been protected and easy. We must at least admire it as a triumphant declaration of faith in life, forged in experience and maintained against prolonged and many-sided adversity.

No man can reach so majestic a conviction by any sudden act of will. He must approach it by stages, as experience of God enriches his mind and soul. And we make a good beginning if we deeply and understandingly believe that *all things work*. This is no more than psychological insight, but it adds meaning to experience. Nothing, literally nothing, that happens to us is futile, ineffectual, meaningless. Every act a man does, every thought that flits across his mind, every emotion or experience is registered somewhere in the fibres of personality, and can under the right circumstances be recalled.

The comment that we were never the same after some great event in life might be made at the end of every common day. We are a part of all that we have met, and all that we have met becomes a part of us. In the lifelong fashioning of the soul everything — tears, laughter, disappointments, delights, moods, holidays, failures, omissions — helps to make us what in the end we are, the end-product of our nature, our faith and our temperament as worked upon by the things we have said and done, enjoyed and reacted against, been entertained by or disgusted by, initiated or been subject to, loved or loathed. All things work, and their effect is never wholly lost.

To this elementary psychology the philosopher's comprehensiveness and sense of proportion add that *all things work together*. Memory is selective, and most people have a strange capacity for judging life mainly by the less pleasant elements of experience. To see life steadily and see it whole brings a deeper insight.

As it takes sun and rain, storm and calm, heat and cold, together to give the oak its toughness; as the different instruments in an orchestra, the different voices in a choir, the varied values in a picture, together hold the secret of beauty, so joy and sorrow, pain and gladness, the things understood and welcomed and the things not understood and secretly resented, together fashion the strong and lovely soul. Most of us have played at some time with those fascinating toys — kaleidoscopes — and their ever-changing patterns of unbelievable intricacy, colour and beauty, until one day the whole thing broke apart in our hands and the ugly bits of broken glass and tinsel scattered to the floor, useless and tawdry. Together, shot through with the light of a divine purpose and love, the bits of life show balance and beauty: alone each single experience may be strange, unlovely and perplexing.

It sounds simple, but it is hard to remember when the need arises that in the total process of fashioning a character one day's tears balance another day's rapture; one hour's pain heightens another hour's pleasure; that success would not thrill if you had never known failure; and that even the high hours of spiritual ecstasy could not by themselves make a saint without other hours of discipline, duty and instructive darkness. For all things work together.

But to the facts of psychology and the wisdom of philosophy must still be added the Christian insight into God's purpose before Paul's great conviction is reached. For the apostle declares also that the total result, the final consequence, is good — for them that love God.

To understand both the assertion and the limitation we must give full weight to Paul's word "good". All things work to promote *goodness,* not happiness, or prosperity, or ease, or the success of our self-chosen schemes, but *goodness.* The great design that controls the pattern of God's providence, God's great end in all that He sends or does, permits or asks of us, is our moral perfection. And the pattern is plain: that we should be conformed to the image of His Son, that He might be, not alone in the universe in solitary unshared perfection, but the First-born among many brethren sharing His likeness.

That breath-taking goal is the whole key to God's providence. It is also the aim of all spiritual progress — "Till we all come, in the unity of the faith, to a perfect man, unto the measure of the stature of the fullness of Christ." It is the highest end in all worship: "For beholding as in a glass the glory of the Lord, we are changed into the same image, from glory to glory, even as by the Spirit of the Lord." And it is the final expectation of the Christian hope: "It doth not yet appear what we shall be, but we know that when he shall appear we shall be like him." Small wonder then that Paul declares this is the purpose towards which all things in life conspire together.

Nor is it strange that this can be true only for those who love upon His grace, and lie unresenting in his hands. The same experiences will embitter, and harden, and warp another soul: but those who love God accept His purpose as their purpose, cooperate with His design, lean upon His wisdom and find their comfort in His care. To such the deepest sorrow can bring a clearer insight and surer hope, the sharpest pain can bring new patience and quiet strength, the greatest disappointment evoke unsuspected fortitude and courage, and the way of the cross make the soul more Christlike.

It is no easy, shallow optimism, but an enlightening and sustaining faith that all things work together for good to make them that love God Christlike.

35 Newness All the Way

THEORETICALLY, the one thing hard to forgive in any preacher of the gospel is staleness. In practice, he often has much excuse, and deserves much sympathy. But however hard pressed he himself may be, at least his message abounds with novelty. It is the story of God's doing "a new thing in the earth". It is *news* of Him who makes all things new. It offers to men the perpetual freshness of eternal morning — "the morning star".

If any man be in Christ there has happened a new creation: that is Paul's astonishing summary of conversion-experience.

He and his world are back in Genesis 1; now for the first time all things are of God —

> *Heaven above is softer blue,*
> *Earth around is sweeter green:*
> *Something breathes in every hue*
> *Christless eyes have never seen:*
> *Birds with gladder songs o'erflow,*
> *Flowers with deeper beauties shine,*
> *Since I know, as now I know,*
> *I am His and He is mine.*

And within, as without, all things are new: a "new man" has replaced the "old", and for a new man only new raiment is becoming — the "garments of the renewed soul" of Colossians 3:12-14. Moreover, the fresh beginning is not upon the old level of existence: the convert is born from above, a freshly minted personality in a new world of experience. God who at the first creation caused the light to shine out of darkness "has done it again".

Thus the gospel is "news" in every sense, new tidings of a fresh start on a new level with new people. Hence our baptism is full of the sense of novelty — a baptism of *regeneration* and *renewing* of the Holy Ghost. We have been planted together, in baptism, in the likeness of Christ's death, that, like as Christ was raised from the dead, we also should walk in newness of life. Baptism, it would here seem, witnesses not merely to what has happened in us, but to what is happening and will go on happening, freshly, always being renewed, to the end of the road.

"Walk in newness": the phrase invites reflection. It plainly suggests that the newness does not wear off, that novelty should attend the whole journey. Intellectually, for a healthy Christian life this must be so. "Be not conformed to this world, but be ye transformed by the renewing of your mind . . ." surely implies that the renewing must be as constant, as reiterated, as unending, as the "not being conformed". But how unfamiliar that emphasis is with us!

We value the settled conviction, the sure mind, the unswerving, unchanging faith, and rightly so. But this also is true, that the man who listens to God must be forever rethinking some things, learning and relearning new truths of God's ways, probing, revising and exploring in the continual endeavour to keep up with the living God, the onward-moving Christ. Not all our loyalty to the written Word, the sacred history, the faith once given to the saints, or to our great tradition, should ever so bind the believing mind fast to ancient things that the guidance of the Spirit in each new age must pass him by, leaving him behind.

But the intellectual renewing must be such as transforms the life. Such is the burden of another apostolic injunction, about the new man's being renewed after the image of Him who created him. "Being renewed", not *was* renewed: for here the muscles of character are constantly being stretched, the horizons of the soul's vision are ever being lifted, the "unsuspected obligations of the Christian life" are gradually being revealed.

Just as we think we have attained, some new vista of duty, some new height of moral possibility, opens before us, and we feel again that we are only beginning to follow Christ. We seem to do no more than press toward an ever-receding target, in obedience to an unlimited, because always upward, call of God in Christ. The fact is that when the *whole* truth is told Christians are not simply born, or made, but always in the process of becoming.

But, of course, discipleship is more than possession of a right faith and pursuit of a true ideal. It is a perpetual inspiration, a continual renewal of the sources of being. Again Paul defines the unending newness: "though the outward man perish, yet the inward man is renewed day by day . . . ." "Outward", here means all the world-contacting side of life, the tiring body, the wearying mind, the frayed nerves, feelings of tension and of conflict, despondency, disappointment. In so many ways the inward strength is drawn upon, and unless we find unfailing springs of spiritual replenishment, the living of these days exhausts us.

But talking to the woman of Samaria, Jesus promised not the incidental cup by the occasional well as we journey, but "in him a well of water, springing up into everlasting life". Walking on with Jesus, into any year, into any new experience, refreshment of soul keeps pace with enlargement of mind and advancing ideals. Nothing grows stale. In an age which seemed to be nearing its end, in a society redolent of decay, the strange evocative promise is recorded: I will give him the Morning Star. Because in His company it is always morning, and newness all the way.

36 Simplicity in Christ

MOST modern versions of the scriptures have got rid of the phrase, "the simplicity that is in Christ", which once translated a remark of Paul's in his second letter to Corinth. "Single devotion, sincerity, single-mindedness" is the idea that takes its place, and we shall not quarrel. Yet the dictionaries give "simplicity" as the first meaning of the word Paul used. This is appropriate because he was contrasting the attitude of mind he wanted the Corinthians to display with the subtlety and cunning of the serpent's temptation of Eve. It is obvious that *subtlety* and *simplicity* are the opposite poles of Paul's argument!

Of course it is dangerous to stress too much the simplicities of faith. The gospel presents the profoundest and most challenging system of thought that the mind of man has wrestled with, and we do well to explore its profundities. Shallowness of faith and understanding leaves Christians vulnerable to every fashionable heresy and fad, and we do well to avoid it. To fail to appreciate the faith we profess is to be useless in service, without witness or influence or testimony to Christ. Far too often a false simplicity passes among us for deep faith when it merely covers up intellectual hypocrisy, spiritual ignorance, and laziness of mind.

The "simple gospel" is often a jumble of Hebrew-Christian conceptions couched in words we use only in church. One remembers Paul's repeated "I would not have you ignorant"; and the appeal in the Letter to the Hebrews that we leave behind the first principles of the gospel of Christ; and Jesus' reproachful question, "How is it that ye do not understand?"

We must not defend a wilful stupidity and emptiness of mind by miscalling it "simplicity".

Yet, when all this is said, an opposite danger remains. We moderns are tempted to delight in complexities, we emit a smoke-screen of discussion and alternative definitions, of complicated argument and many-sided questions, to hide us from the duty of making up our minds. We live in a fog of half-explanations, a maze of theories that contradict each other; we make every issue of faith and conduct a matter for enquiry until we lose the reality of the Christian life in all the talk about it. Often we cannot see the truth for thinking, and we cannot hear our conscience speak because we are arguing so loudly.

Then simplicity pleads to be heard. It is a thing of character as well as of mind, of understanding as well as of speech, of conscience as well as of faith. And often it finds the way while the experts are finding their maps.

For the things a man *must* know are few and plain. To do justly, love mercy, and walk humbly with our God is not easy to do but is simple to *understand*: and Micah says it is what the Lord requires. Isaiah puts the timeless divine invitation in words of one or two syllables (with two easy exceptions): "Seek ye the Lord while he may be found, call ye upon him while he is near; let the wicked forsake his way, and the unrighteous man his thoughts, and let him return unto the Lord, and he will have mercy upon him, and to our God, for he will abundantly pardon."

"Believe on the Lord Jesus Christ, and thou shalt be saved" is clear enough counsel, even though it means setting out under sealed orders on a life of endless surrender. And "Come unto me", "Follow me", "I have given you an example" are not commands we fail to obey for want of understanding.

But we *like* complexity. The Corinthians preferred a sensational, exciting, ecstatic experience of prophecies and visions and tongues and trances to the humdrum business of belief and behaviour that apostolic instruction emphasised. To know God was surely an unearthly wisdom; to possess the divine Spirit was to live on the edge of things magic and mysterious; the odd and abnormal and emotional were the proofs that one was spiritual — and the grounds of pride. But their everyday life in Corinth left much to be desired. No wonder Paul insisted they return to the simplicities of faith.

The Roman Christians, too, liked complexity: some argumentation and Christian philosophy, a little of the fantastic and clever. They would climb high above for heavenly lore and dig deep in hidden wisdom and archaic language or roam far in search of distant cultures and alien religions. Paul seems to have all this in mind as he quotes to them an ancient text with Christian comment: "Do not say in your heart, 'Who will ascend into heaven?' (that is, to bring Christ down) or 'Who will descend into the abyss?' (that is, to bring Christ up from the dead). . . . The word is near you, on your lips and in your heart . . . because, if you confess with your lips that Jesus is Lord and believe in your heart that God raised him from the dead, you will be saved." In the last resort, it is simplicity that saves.

And Peter, too, liked complexity. The Lord's enquiry concerning his love, the threefold commission to feed the flock, the warning of tests ahead and the renewed command to follow — these should have been enough. But Peter is aware of wider implications, of social duties, of problems of the inter-relation of Christians, of complications that arise in varying minds, and of unusual circumstances. "Lord," he asks, concerning John's discipleship, "what shall this man do?" There are times when Jesus Himself must call us back to simplicity and relevance in unmistakable terms: "What is that to thee? Follow thou me!"

37 Symbols of the Spirit

WE abandon a little too easily the attempt to understand what happened at Pentecost. Content with a series of contrasts, between disciples afraid, sad, silent and confined within locked doors one moment, and fearless, rejoicing, articulate, and free a little later, we tend to say, "This is the difference the Spirit made; what made this difference was the Spirit", and we let it go at that. Neither the meaning nor the promise of the gift of the Spirit is as well understood as the story of Bethlehem or the message of the cross: and we are the poorer for assuming we shall never understand it.

Of course, the ultimate explanations are hidden in eternal wisdom. Yet revelation makes (so to speak) a particular effort to render Pentecost intelligible by employing three metaphors familiar and homely to non-theological minds. It all had to do with wind and fire and tongues — and what person who has felt the wind on his face, or warmed his hands by the fire, or spoken with his friends, can pretend *these* things are beyond him?

Set between desert and sea, Palestine knew winds and feared them, as much as any land. To the west, the winds lifted the waters and poured them out on the land, whipping the sea into sudden storms such as inspired the writer of Psalm 107. To the east they drove the hot sand for miles across the desert, destroying all living things, burying the landmarks and, all too often, the unwary traveller too. To the north, the forest of Lebanon bore testimony to the tearing force that could (in the words of Psalm 29) "make Lebanon skip like a calf . . . make the oaks to whirl, and strip the forests bare". In the wilderness of the south, the wind howling about the bare mountains (or through the Jordan valley) seems to have earned the nickname of Night Siren, or Roarer.

This habit of naming the winds Sirocco, or Euroclydon, betrays the half-superstitious fear inspired by the invisible power whose effects could be seen in wind and sand and storm but whose cause and path remained a mystery. Clouds raced, mountains shook, the Sea of Galilee's waves lashed the shores and shivered to pieces the frail fishing craft: yet nothing was seen of the hand that did it. It was a natural dynamic, a fierce "anger", like that of mighty men which imparted "life" to inanimate things and made them menacing. And in man himself, in gentler form, the wind of breath was the invariable accompani-

106

ment of life: the wind, or breath, of God Himself had made man a living soul.

In the grim vision of Ezekiel, the *wind* from the four corners of the earth imparts life to the dry bones of an ancient battle-field and restores a mighty army.

Power invisible and irresistible, life unseen but mighty — this the wind means, and is: and at Pentecost a rushing, mighty wind filled all the house where they were sitting.

Flames "sat upon each of them." John had promised a baptism of fire as part of Messiah's judgement in the earth. Somewhere behind his words is the echo of Isaiah's great prophecy of the purging of the blood of Jerusalem by a blast (or wind — again suggesting "spirit") of judgement, a blast of burning. So the Christ (John said) would come as a forest fire driving the snakes before it; as a farmer thoroughly sweeping his threshing floor and burning the chaff with unquenchable fire.

The language is hardly that which we would apply to Jesus, but it had a long and intelligible tradition behind it. In the judgement of Sodom, in the flames and smoke of Sinai, in the pale reflection of both that burned unceasingly on the Temple altar, the purging, cleansing power of fire is ascribed to the holy presence of God. In the metaphor of Malachi, the purifying virtue of fire is enshrined in the figure of the divine Refiner, who bends above the crucible in which the precious metal of His people is being assayed until by His own reflection on the surface He knows it is pure.

And so at Pentecost the Spirit of holiness, that maketh pure, appeared as flame, to refine or to consume, as man shall choose.

The third metaphor of Pentecost has a double reference that almost amounts to a pun. The flaming tongues that sat upon each person find first expression in the loosened tongues that suddenly become articulate and free in the proclamation of the gospel. The first of all manifestations of the Spirit in the Church was a sermon! The will to communicate, the message to be communicated, the boldness to communicate it fearlessly, these the Spirit gave to the disciples. In the knowledge of the truth, the ability to expound it, and the desire to share it, His presence in the Church has ever been made known. For He is the Spirit of truth — truth known, truth uttered, and truth proclaimed.

At Pentecost Christianity became "alive". Before Pentecost it comprised a teaching, an Example, a love for a Person. Now it became a world movement, a history-changing faith. The secret then and now is set forth sufficiently in wind and fire and tongues: for He is the Spirit of Power, and Purity, and everlasting Truth.

38 Bracing Comfort

OUT of a mildly funny description of a poor home-town in an industrial backwater hit by the years of depression, there leaped an acid sentence. It describes the Sunday mornings, with no work to be tired of or to look forward to, and with no money to spend the week-end away: "Back-gardens full of bored men smoking . . . a hush upon the main street . . . no buses, no nothing . . . except the measured tread of the solace-seekers heading for the churches . . . ."

Of course it was easy for a successful journalist in an affluent society to poke fun at the faith of people facing poverty and fear and emptiness of life, an adversity and a blankness ahead such as he (largely through their steadfastness and faith and sacrifice) had never known. Easy and cheap, but nevertheless that was a picture he believed in: Christians as solace-seekers, turning to the churches as the child to its comforter, seeking in God a magnified father-figure with strong arms and a firm shoulder to cry upon.

A faint element of truth lingers in the caricature. The modern world is a fairly frightening place in which to live, and men and women of religious faith have no need to apologise to a generation that seeks its own consolation in noise, drink, drugs, space-fiction, sexual hysteria, erotic fiction, morbid horror and the artificial excitements of gambling. It is not the seeking of consolation, but the source to which he turns, that reveals the man. The truth is that religious comfort has a bracing, searching, demanding quality that befits a truly adult mind.

"Comfort ye, comfort ye my people, saith your God. Speak ye comfortably to Jerusalem, and cry unto her . . . ." *What?* Wherein lies the comfort the prophet is commanded to bring to a people humiliated, defeated, in exile, far from home, without freedom and without hope? What is he to say?

This for one thing: "Say unto her that her iniquity is pardoned; she hath received of the Lord's hand double for all her sins." Pardon, mercy, reconciliation for a people stricken in conscience and laden with guilt to the point of despair: this is consolation indeed. But it is not soft. The exile has been a stern lesson; Israel has drunk a bitter medicine; she has received all she asked for. If now she may return and start again, it is not because God is careless of evil and condones wrong. This is a world where evil matters and God deals with it; where as a man sows, so shall he reap; where morality is fundamental, built into the frame of things; and where, though mercy triumphs in the end, it is neither cheap, nor blind, nor stupid. That is strong comfort, indeed; for our deepest fear of all is that there might be no fundamental right, no final judgement, in a universe blind to evil and to good.

Say to her this, for a second thing: "Prepare ye the way of the Lord . . . make straight a highway for our God. Every mountain shall be exalted . . . the crooked be made straight . . . the glory of the Lord shall be revealed . . . ." Babylon seems invincible, the future looks bleak, the entire outlook is hopeless. But great things are going on, new things are happening, changes are on the way, for *God is astir*. Return and renewal are at hand. A corner is reached. History is ready to move forward again in the purpose of God. A quickening comfort there! Nothing makes faith droop and resolution fade like the fear that the world is drifting helplessly out of control, that it is blindly driven by impersonal forces with no hand at the helm. Yet to believe that God is astir offers no cheap comfort: it demands that we bestir ourselves, and prepare His way.

Say to her this, for a third thing: "All flesh is grass, and all the goodliness thereof as the flower of the field. . . . The grass withereth, the flower fadeth; but the word of our God shall stand for ever." What is human is transient. Man's pride and error and folly all pass away; man's opposition to God's purpose withers and dies. Only the Word and the will of God endure. Nothing so desolates Christian hearts as much as the lurking doubt whether all the great things once believed in — God's character and love, God's kingdom and grace, God's judgement and salvation, God's invitation and promise — are still true today. The answer is that God has spoken, and none shall contradict Him. His Word endures when all else changes. Firm comfort there! His Word is our peace and law.

Say this to Jerusalem, for a fourth thing . . . , then there follows a wonderful passage, among the finest in all literature, affirming in matchless poetry and noble, persuasive argument, the sovereignty of God. He rules in the strength of His arm, yet is He tender in His might. He is Maker of the worlds, measuring out the heavens, weighing the hills, calculating the dust of the earth — a marvellous flight of imagination that sets the poet in Genesis 1 watching God at His work. He is infinite in counsel, in justice, in understanding; Ruler of the nations and the scattered islands of the sea; beyond all adequate worship — Lebanon's forest and all its beasts are not sacrifice sufficient! His glory defies description, belittles all comparison. God sits enthroned above the arch of heaven, stretching out the blue for the curtain of His tent, controlling on earth the destinies of great peoples, moving princes like stubble before the wind, marshalling the very stars as His forces for victory. *God reigns.* Man struts and fumes and shouts, or cowers in fear and dread of his own folly; but God's wit runs through the earth. Men's freedom has fixed limits. Man can disobey but cannot get away with it; he can defy, but God bends his defiance to His own purpose in the end. God reigns: bracing comfort there! — so long as you are on God's side.

Say this for a final thing: that this mighty and sovereign God has time and strength and patience for individual men. No man's way is hid from the Lord, no man's cause passed over.

The everlasting God fainteth not, neither is weary: "He giveth power to the faint, and to them that have no might he increaseth strength." Though even young men fall, they that wait on the Lord shall renew their strength, mount up with wings, run without weariness, walk without collapse. For the greatness of God is grace to His people, and they that wait on Him are strong. Deep comfort there, if you believe.

This is the quality of religious comfort. A world with morality and mercy at the heart of it, purpose behind it, enduring certainty within it, God above it, and strength available to conquer it. This is strong comfort that increases a man's stature, establishes the soul, challenges the best in him, uplifts the heart, and widens the horizons of his thought and endeavour.

It is certainly no anaesthetic for moral weaklings sneering at consolation!

39 Keeping the Outsider Inside

IN I Corinthians 14 Paul touches upon a subject almost too sore, in these last years, for temperate discussion. In briefest terms, it is the problem of relating evangelistic campaigns to established church life. It is the urgent need that every soul-winning enterprise shall be backed by a corresponding zeal to welcome the new converts to their place within existing Christian fellowships. It means not just follow-up, but follow-in. It is a troublesome business.

Somewhat unexpectedly, Paul criticised the kind of meetings that were held at Corinth. Even more startling is the basis of his judgment. "What would the chance outsider, coming in, make of what you do? What would a stranger think? How much would he be profited, or helped, or edified — how much would he understand?" Look at your church programme through his eyes and imagine his reactions! It is a sobering suggestion.

A man in middle life, genuinely disturbed and anxious to learn the Christian way, accepted wise advice and joined a local church in order to learn by doing. After six months he summarised his impressions: "A fine body of people, earnest, sincere, friendly, generous, hard-working . . . but I am not one whit wiser about the essence of the Christian faith or the practice of the Christian life."

We know, immediately, that it was a Protestant church he tried, probably a non-credal church, and likelier one in Britain than in America! But that church, whatever and wherever it was, had only obeyed the countless injunctions repeated inside and outside the church for thirty years: the demand for short, snappy sermons, practical and not doctrinal, above all easy to listen to and easy to forget, entertaining, but never profound, for a church life of social occasions and varied interests, not religion all the time. And so a hungry soul was turned away unfed.

At the opposite extreme is the kind of church that is grounded in the Word of God, keenly evangelical, zealously engaged in devotional, evangelistic, missionary activity, tending to reduce Christianity to a series of "meetings", content to let the world and the worldling pass it by. Often praying indeed, "Lord send the outsiders in", but adding in a fervent undertone, "But, Lord, let them be our sort".

In the increasing evangelistic fervour of our day this problem of adjusting existing church routines to keep the outsider in — if ever he comes in — grows in importance. Paul insists that we expect him, cater for him, and consider his point of view. He may be a friend, a neighbour, a former member long out of touch, or a visitor from overseas. He may be a stranger, a shabby stranger, perhaps a morally shabby stranger; but we hold *public* worship, and we are a redeemed and redeeming society, or we are nothing at all. The sharpest criticism, and saddest comment, applying to any church is that it is the last place to which the lonely, the wretched, the remorseful, the despairing, would think to turn.

The effort demanded is many-sided. Paul uses two words that suggest where effort might begin. He speaks continually in this connection of "the unlearned" and "the unbeliever". The latter, presumably, is the outsider who knows, but is unconvinced. He has some Christian background and the basic information, but he does not vitally or eagerly believe. For him it is necessary that his tenuous ideas should "come alive" in the fervour, friendliness, and plain sincerity of the Church. He needs to be challenged by the difference he observes between himself and others and comforted by the quality of life into which the Church has drawn him. But how shall this be done? Church friendships are already formed, the young people are paired off, and homes and firesides already booked by visiting habits of long standing. It is a heart-stretching exercise, this continual re-arrangement of our social patterns to absorb continual newcomers. This is "follow-in"!

The other case is harder still. He does not know what our worship is all about — our Bible in archaic language, our odd hymns and poetic prayer, our half-conscious motives and unconscious assumptions are all foreign to him. What a colossal effort of mental adjustment we require of those who come amongst us fashioned by cinema morality, school science, and glossy magazines! Our basic conceptions of God, of ethics, of history, life and purpose, are all new and strange ideas to many modern minds. How far do we make ourselves easier to understand? The first necessity of evangelism is not excitement, nor publicity, but intelligibility.

Of course, it requires for the pulpit more freedom to deal with topics and talk in language not usually heard in Christian worship. It demands an equally serious effort over the whole area of church affairs to shape our services, our prayers, our conversation *and our hearts* with the enquiring outsider in our view. The reward is high: the outsider "is convinced . . . judged . . . the secrets of his heart made manifest . . . he will worship God, and report that God is among you of a truth . . .".

40 The Answer

JOHN sent to Jesus a theological enquiry: about the right title to be applied to Him, about the true interpretation of prophecy, about the due order of divine events. "Art thou he that should come, or do we look for another?" Jesus replied, not with a definition, a lecture, a sermon, or even a parable, but with *news* — a description of things happening. "Go and show John again those things which ye do hear and see: the blind receive their sight, and the lame walk, the lepers are cleansed, and the deaf hear, the dead are raised up, and the poor have the gospel preached to them." "Art Thou the King?" Show John the kingdom in action, and let him judge for himself.

Thus Jesus submits to the test of truth and falsehood which He proposed for others. Truth may be assessed by deeds, the tree by its fruit, faith by character, doctrine by obedience, religion by life. There is no argument so cogent as action. Whether it be adulation of Himself as "Lord, Lord . . ." without corresponding surrender, or ostentatious leaves on a barren tree, or the insight given into the heart by examination of its "overflow" in speech, or the prefiguring of final judgement by charity and compassion, always the emphasis of Jesus falls upon the proof of claims by deeds, of profession by actual accomplishment. So when John asks, "Art Thou the King?" Jesus answers not with claims or argument or doctrine but with, "Shew him what I do: the blind receive their sight, the lame walk, the lepers are cleansed . . .".

So deeds matter. They are not merely evidence but concrete vehicles of meaning and truth. Actions reveal with dramatic force the assumptions, attitudes, principles and aims of him who acts. The events reported back to John are not listed at random but are such as enshrine the inmost meaning of the kingdom John awaits. This that he sees *is* the King at work. This is the kind of King He is. This is the nature of His rule. This is the divine philanthropy. In Acts 18, that modern-sounding word describes the "simple humanity" of certain barbarians towards the shipwrecked companions of Paul, but in Titus 3 it is daringly applied to God, as summarising the very heart of His revelation of Himself in Christ: the "simple humanity" of God!

The point would not be lost upon John, for just here lay his whole difficulty. He had proclaimed an imminent Messiah with axe and shovel, flail and fire. Instead, Jesus appeared with (to speak in terms of modern medical missions) bandages and anaesthetics, herbs and a healing touch, with compassion, and stories, and the proclamation not of judgement but of love. To this extent John had got it wrong and might yet so easily "stumble". Judgement there must be, but the fundamental thing is love, the divine "humanity". Messiah has come, not merely to burn chaff and chop down trees, but that the blind might receive their sight, the lame walk, the unclean be cleansed. This *is* the gospel, and the deeds of Jesus give it visible and substantial embodiment.

That in itself makes the answer of Jesus to John a significant comment upon all attempts to reduce the gospel to right opinions and an orthodox creed.

John was, of course, thinking in larger terms, too. Some would say he was thinking "dispensationally". He sees Jesus against a wide canvas of ancient hopes and prophecies and his own announcement of the climax of the ages. John is thinking of the Messiah as the turning-point in God's time-sweeping purposes, as confronting not that age alone but all the ages. "Look we for another?" — "Tell John, the blind receive their sight, the lame walk . . .".

Here, if John could but see it, is the glorious fulfilment of the prophets' dream of a better world, of healing and peace, of plenty and joy. Here, in the deeds of Jesus, is the promised outflow of stupendous power in victorious conflict with demonic forces that dispute God's reign. Here is the Saviour who should take not only man's infirmities but also his sins, and bear them upon Himself. Here, in the deeds of Jesus, is evidence, expression, and expectation of the kingdom that is to be. John need look no further: God's actions speak louder than words.

115

Is not this still the only answer to questions like John's, to men's enquiries about the ultimate truth of Christianity? Missionary reviews are filled with warnings of rising nationalism in south and east; of old faiths reawakening, in intellectual vigour, moral ardour, and missionary zeal. From centuries of comparative slumber and assumed acceptance, heathenism experiences its own revival under the stimulus of communism, scepticism, and perhaps of envy. What is our answer to the heathen challenge?

The story of a manger and a cross? Yes, undoubtedly, but they have their own sacred stories. The holy scriptures? By all means, but they have their own authoritative books. Our answer must still be truth made eloquent in deeds. It must be the answer of love made credible by loving hands and hearts: doctors, teachers, nurses, relief workers, administrators, scientists, dieticians, technologists, and the rest, active evangelists of a faith whose best expression is in concrete kindness. These are our answer. And what to do about the H-bomb and the ancient hate? How do we succour the starving and the refugee and the hungry, awakening mind? As the rising peoples of the twentieth century send their question to Jesus, the only answer they will hear, believe, or understand will be that made in the Master's form: "The blind receive their sight, the lame walk, the lepers are cleansed, to the poor good news is preached."

41 The Ark of God

SCRIPTURE tells two somewhat similar stories about the Ark of Israel and the uses to which it might be put. The difference between them gives food for thought. The sacred chest, overlaid with gold, and reputed to contain Aaron's rod and an earthen pot of manna, enshrined for the pious Jew stirring memories of the desert wandering of his fathers in the great days of the Exodus. In the wilderness Tabernacle, later at Shiloh, and later still at Jerusalem, it became "the mercy seat", throne and symbol of the presence in Israel of her invisible God. Once a year, on the great Day of Atonement, it became the place of confession and expiation of the whole nation's sin.

During the Philistine raids in the days of Eli, the Ark was taken from the shrine at Shiloh to the front line of battle, the people seeking, in some sense, to carry their religion (or their God) forth to their daily life and conflict. It did not work. They lost the battle, as before. They lost the Ark. And they lost Eli, their priest, so that henceforth, until Samuel arose, God was silent and inaccessible. Over that day's triple tragedy an infant's awful name was written: Ichabod — the glory has departed!

What then was wrong? Is it not a good thing to carry faith and religious principle forth from the sheltered sanctuary into the front line of everyday life? How are we to interpret the story or to explain its preservation in the Hebrew scriptures?

The essential point is clearly Israel's insincerity. The last chapters of the book of Judges portray the time: a wayward generation, an age undisciplined, worship fouled with vice, the old priest weak and the young priests wicked. Such were the people, such was the time, that sought to use the Ark of God to prosecute their war.

God is no man's tool. The attempt to use religion for our own ends never succeeds, whether it be to promote our business by parade of piety, to gather morale through crisis-days of prayer, to rise on religious reputation to political eminence, or to preserve democracy by evangelism. Trailing the Ark of God at the wheels of *our* chariots means that the Ark will surely be lost and the chariot ultimately destroyed. Whether it be clerics using spiritual prestige to wield secular power, or diplomats claiming a religious basis for their policy while issuing threats of wholesale indiscriminate destruction, the attempt to manipulate religion for private gain is always the sure prelude to Ichabod.

When you take the Ark of God to battle, it is well to be sure that the battle is the Lord's and that your hands are clean.

Must we then always leave the Ark safe at Shiloh, separating the sacred altar and the holy fire from the world's affairs? Must we fold our hands in prayer, keeping them unsullied in idleness lest we stain them with the grime of a troubled and often sordid environment? Not, certainly, while the Old Testament prophets remain a part of the Christian scriptures, exclaiming against worship divorced from commerce and politics, the market place and the courthouse. Not, certainly, while the four Gospels show us Jesus bringing faith and piety, religion and the rule of God, to bear directly upon everyday concerns.

No, the Ark *must* be carried forth into the world's conflicts, into factory and office, to workbench and school, along the high-roads of life's progress. So runs the second story, with the Ark again in the front line as priests and Levites bear it in solemn procession around the walls of Jericho. This time the stratagem succeeds: the city falls, the land and the future lie open for Israel's occupation.

This time it is different. The Ark leads the way; priests and elders, soldiers and people, *follow* the Ark in obedience to divine command. This time the battle is the Lord's, the land a place for His possession, and Israel enters, as Joshua reminds them, only as His servants. This time the restraint of the divine will forbids private plunder or revenge; all is devoted to Jehovah alone.

The world itself can see the difference, can sense the great gulf between the Christian with a social conscience and the politician or the businessman with a religious gimmick. If Christians profess concern about world affairs and social wrongs only in pursuit of their own interests, men contemptuously reject their counsel and their faith. If we can show a true compassion, a disinterested anxiety for the welfare of society, they will surely think again. When we encompass with our faith the entrenched forces of evil in the conviction that the earth, *and we,* are the Lord's, then the Ark of His presence will lead us in triumph and the kingdoms of this world become the kingdom of our God. Unfortunately, it is deceptively easy to identify the Lord's interests with our own and passionately to believe we are calling men to fight the Lord's battles when we are merely blowing our own trumpet.

42 A Seaside Parable

NIGHT crossing was never very pleasant on that stretch of water. A head-on wind was boisterous and the ship made heavy going. She was a small craft, probably somewhat over-laden, and the atmosphere on board was perhaps not all it might have been.

The lake was the Sea of Galilee, and they were *toiling in rowing*. Since several of the rowers were lifelong fishermen, ac-customed to the vagaries of wind and water, the phrase is striking: even they found it wearying work. Doubtless the few who knew nothing of the sea were telling the experts how it should be done, or getting in the way, and the experts all the more sensitive to criticism because they knew they should be going faster! Tired, discouraged, frustrated men tend to be quarrelsome, are easily upset.

Besides, *the wind was contrary*, and this added to the difficul-ties of keeping the ship's prow head-on. Progress, such as it was, seemed vacillating and confused. It meant no sail, no outside help, no offer of respite to the weary muscles. Every inch of gain must be won against wind and current by strength of sinew and unrelenting strain. A favorable breeze of revival (or even of publicity, which is not *quite* the same thing) can help so much.

And *it was night*. They were in the dark about many things. The turn of events puzzled them. The day behind had seen a glorious miracle and mounting enthusiasm to make the Master king. But He had withdrawn Himself and even now is absent; and they are making for the other side of the lake, for no apparent reason, leaving success behind. What with weariness, frustration, and misgivings, their hearts were hardly in it!

It was a small ship. With the work hard, the wind con-trary, the way perplexing, the crew not too united — it might have been a small-town church, or a downtown cause in some great city, or a tiny mission station making little headway, or a pioneering venture from which the first enthusiasm had long since died away. There had been years when things sailed smoothly, a fair wind filled the sails, the oars kept time with each other, the sun of blessing shone on calm waters and progress could be measured by numbers gained and great occasions vividly remembered. But since the leaders died — since the war — since the population drifted elsewhere — since the quarrel — it has been all toiling in rowing, the wind contrary, the tide against us, and the future dark.

Yet these men were in the will of Christ. He had sent them at that time to do that task. We must beware, in these hedonistic days, of that shallow Christian optimism which stupidly assumes that when the heart is right and a true course is being steered, the wind and water will be in our favour, cheering crowds will line the banks, and the holds will burst with the abundant catch. The modern cult of "come to Jesus and be happy, relaxed, prosperous, successful, popular at parties, integrated to a higher degree of personality-magnetism" is a shoddy business beside the heroic faith that dared men to take up the discipline and dedication of the cross and follow Christ through peril, toil, and pain.

Truly consecrated service can mean hardship, disappointment, and perplexity. Jonah found a boat waiting, the fare in his pocket; but that was when he would run away from God's appointed task. A fair wind deceived the captain of Paul's ship into a voyage that proved disastrous. There is little doubt that many were ready to offer the prodigal a lift to the far country, though few would help the penniless lad on his way home again. On the other hand, Paul went bound in the Spirit to Jerusalem, where bonds and imprisonment awaited him; and his own settled expectation — which he shared candidly even with young converts — that "through many tribulations we must enter the kingdom of God", is wholly in line with the Master's warnings that the gateway to life is narrow, that he who will not take up his cross cannot be a disciple, and that he who thinks to embark upon the Christian warfare does well first to sit down and think if he can see it through.

However hard the toil, or contrary the wind, or dark the night, we must be at pains to keep a place in the boat for Christ. It is fatally easy to brood on the disappointments, the heart clouded with self-pity, fellowship spoiled by lingering resentments against fancied, or real, disloyalties. It is easy, too, in our envy of more "successful" colleagues, to criticise experiments we have not tried, to pour scorn upon new methods, to find unworthy explanations of another's progress. Then, when the Lord draws near across the darkened, wind-swept waters, we are found unready, even afraid, almost letting the Master pass us by.

Yet each thing said of Jesus in this story is exquisite. He saw them and knew their toil. He came to them — He always does. He talked with them: "Be of good cheer!" He entered the ship and the wind ceased. H. M. Stanley somewhere says that his African carriers soon wearied, loitered, and were tempted by every fruit tree on the path, until the arrows of the bushmen found them. The chief difficulty in making progress lay in keeping his workers near him.

Perhaps Christ would say the same.

43 "A Lad Here!"

THERE is a lad here." That is the sentence upon which the whole perplexing situation turned. The surging crowd was weary, hungry, far from home. The challenge of Jesus to the Twelve seemed impossible to fulfill. Then someone said, "A lad here!" — and all was well. He was the answer to a problem; that in itself is highly significant. Nowadays we far too frequently assume that young people *are* the problem — with sad justification, sometimes, in city streets, shadowed homes, or exasperated courts. But this youngster was the answer, not the problem; and in that he does not stand alone.

When long years of strife and deep disunity had weakened Israel in the dark days of the judges, when all noble souls despaired of seeing better days, God answered, "There's a lad here!" — Samuel, priest, prophet, king-maker, man of God.

And all was well. When the first king failed, and the people no longer had faith in kings or God, again the answer came, "There's a lad here!" — David, keeping sheep at Bethlehem, God's provision for a needy time. When Europe was torn with confusion and trouble, the Church herself decayed and spiritless, and true hearts everywhere sighed for happier times, God answered yet again, "A lad is here!" and gay, brave and debonair St. Francis stepped forth to follow Christ and draw half Europe after him.

How very, very often God's answer to a problem has been a youngster, full of faith, with heart aflame: Augustine, St. Aidan, a wealthy Quaker girl, Lincoln, Livingstone, Booker Washington, Carey . . . the list is endless. With all reverence we may fancy that high over Bethlehem, through the shuddering darkness of a whole world lost, there sounded once the wondering whisper, "There's a Lad here!" — and the sons of God sang together once again for joy.

In every age God is getting ready, somewhere, His answer to our problems. We have not learned to look on youth with Christian eyes until we see in them God's coming servants, the living promises of a new day and a better time.

Whether the youngster will become a problem, or the answer to a problem — who shall say? The secret lies with Andrew. Without that watchful, self-effacing, faithful disciple, the lad would never have entered the picture. Too often, because there was no one to notice, no one to care, because through the corridors of the church the whisper rang, "These kids!" — it was a police official in the courthouse who solemnly intoned, "There's a lad here"; or a brokenhearted mother and father who shamefully whispered, "Yes, she's our girl."

The youngster, with all life and fun and promise bottled up inside, needs Andrew; someone to notice, someone to care, someone to kick off the slippers, turn off the TV, put on the raincoat and go down the hall to do what he can to show friendless, leaderless youth that Christ cares because Christians care. What a wonderful line of Andrews Jesus has gathered around Him! Barnardo, Quarrier, Raikes, and Francis Clark, Baden Powell and William Smith and Merrell Vories of the Omi

Brotherhood, and hosts of others who, week in and week out, within our churches or on the fringe, give time and strength and leadership and love to seek the lads and girls for Christ.

God multiply their number!

Of course, there must be Someone else. Without Him, the lad is nobody, one among five thousand, part of the problem. Without Him, Andrew is just another of the helpless, arguing disciples, endlessly debating what to do. But when Andrew has the wit, the faith, the personal experience, to bring the lad to Christ, the situation changes. It is not easy to lead youth to Christ. There are many disappointments. Many will be found to criticise, to discourage, and with superb wisdom to ask, "What are these among so many?" But Christ will welcome them, accept their lives and gifts, and by His matchless power achieve great things through those too often disregarded, too soon despaired about.

Salute, then, in St. Andrew's name, the great army of disciples who in the lives of lads and girls about our churches are serving faithfully their Saviour, the kingdom, and the future.

44 The Middle Virtue

HOPE is a guardian of human reason. What lovely things are said in the scriptures of hope!

It saves, for none are so thoroughly lost as those who have lost heart. In illness, temptation, adversity, we are so very often saved simply by believing in tomorrow. Disgrace lies not so much in failure as in despair; the last defeat is not in giving way but in giving up. When strength is gone and prayer is difficult, when faith is weak and vision is clouded, we may yet be "saved by hope" if we but hold out.

It purifies, for to hope for ultimate good is to be nerved and inspirited to pursue. The soul that expects no splendour is soon sullied, seeing evil everywhere and becoming used to it. The heart that believes that the outcome is in God's hands is free from the corroding poisons of cynicism. To look for His appearing is, John says, to purify oneself even as He is pure.

It rejoices, even in tribulation. When nothing in the immediate circumstances warrants joy, hope borrows from the future for the need of today and lights its candle in the evening with the promise of a coming dawn. It matters nothing that it does not see — for what a man seeth, why doth he yet hope for? But not seeing, hope still rejoices; cloudy and disappointing though today might be, tomorrow lies unspoiled in the strong hands of God.

It comforts. When perplexity deepens sorrow, and sadness turns to bitterness, hope is the quiet strength that builds in the inmost heart a place of healing, steadiness, and calm. Far more than we realise, "we sorrow not even as others who have no hope", but comfort one another with words that they alone know who have felt the presence of a risen Lord and have knelt in worship at an empty tomb.

And it abides. Much passes as the years slip by. Much that we set our hearts upon came to us, or did not come: the difference is not always great. Knowledge and emotion lose their excitement, prophecy fails and tongues cease; but faith and love abide and, linking them together, hope remains with us, permanent and unyielding, growing brighter as other things fade, and strengthening in the rays of the setting sun.

Such hope is a *helmet* for the mind beset with doubt. Questions will be answered in God's good time, and arguments dissolved in understanding. Short views of most problems tend to cynicism because the unfinished story often seems the perfect illustration of divine injustice or indifference. But hope's long view corrects the mental vision and guards the believing mind from the wiles of the devil.

Such hope is a *refuge* for the soul when cowardice, fear, despondency assail. The heart needs shelter when cross-winds blow. It is easy to be superior about "escapism", but he is a foolish captain who scorns the harbour in the day of storm.

When the forces ranged against us are too strong, and safety may be purchased without failure of duty, it is plain spiritual sense to "flee for refuge to lay hold upon the hope" within the veil, where storm and conflict cease, and where Christ our Forerunner has already entered, until with renewed strength we can face the blast again. Hope *is* such a refuge. As surely as memory steals fire from the radiance of the past to glorify the present, so does hope steal courage from the victory of the future to steady the soul in the struggles of today.

Such hope is also called an *anchor* for the will, holding the conscience fast against the currents of passion and the tides of popular taste. Lack of a future tense is the undoing of many souls: "Let us eat, drink, and be merry, for tomorrow we die!" Christian foresight nerves the will to steadfastness by adding a new dimension to every situation and a new depth to character, by illuminating all decisions with the clear promise — or warning — of tomorrow's wisdom, regret, and reward.

Such manifold confidence in all coming good is raised on two foundations. On revelation: "For whatsoever things were written aforetime were written for our learning, that we through patience and comfort of the scriptures might have hope." "Hope thou in God" is the message of the Old Testament; "Christ is our hope" is the answer of the New. God, seen and understood in Jesus, is our deepest argument for hopefulness. God is good and undefeated; Christ walked our world serene and sure of foot, with faith unfaltering. That suffices.

Yet revelation is supported by experience, which "worketh hope". Paul denies that experience must bring disillusion. Every hour spent in God's service, every day lived in His presence, every example of His favour that memory accumulates, breeds hope. Unto such living hope were we begotten again, and He that began a good work will perform it until the day of Christ.

uc
iod

45 Full Circle

WE have seen the wheel turn full circle. We knew that our society and way of life had moved far from the days of Uzziah. In Uzziah's day, true religion and high morality went hand in hand, and from that combination sprang the impulse to many great reforms. We had seen Jotham replace Uzziah, as high morality, living on inherited spiritual capital but having no roots in present religious experience, or worship, or faith of its own, kept at least the public life comparatively sweet and clean. We had seen the inevitable result in Ahaz the grandson: morality devoid of religion proving its inability to perpetuate itself or restrain a third generation which boasted its lack of both faith and morals. And we thought the story complete. Morality arising from religion in the first generation; morality inherited from religion in the second; neither morality nor religion in the third: the sequence was familiar.

But a fourth stage is evidently upon us. A famous newspaper prints the following counsel from "a psychologist and sociologist":

> Nothing that the child learns at school up to the age of seven or eight is so important as the moral training he receives. . . . Usually this moral sense is acquired through general religious training. This . . . raises problems for parents who do not belong to any particular church. . . . What matters far more than the kind of religious instruction that can be imparted by a teacher is the attitude that can be built up within the child's mind. The language of religion is ideally suited to this purpose. If the child is told that his bad desires are temptations by the devil it will make sense of what is happening to him. Some parents are worried if they have to teach a child doctrines they themselves do not wholly believe. Yet there is no hypocrisy in addressing a child on his own level. The truths of religion are often best expressed in myths. . . .

What appalling folly.

One should be grateful perhaps that the proportions and potential dangers of delinquency are at last receiving urgent popular attention. One should contrive to be glad that even in irreligious circles the connection of morality and faith is grudgingly beginning to be discerned. But for the conclusions here drawn, what can one have but impatience and scorn?

Is it not a cardinal principle of child-training *never* to tell the child as true things it must later learn to be untrue, lest you betray its trust, destroy its reverence for authority, and undermine its inner intellectual security? Is it not a cardinal principle of morality never to do to others what you hold it wrong for them to do? Would the "acknowledged expert" count it strange if the child so hoodwinked with religious myths to condition it to "right" behaviour should turn upon its mentors with similar guile and tell them — its parents and probation officers — just what it considered good for *them* to think?

Is it not a cardinal principle of science not to reject a hypothesis that works just because its apparent explanation may conflict with intellectual prejudices based on other theories? If it be true that religious training produces the wholesome, social character, why assume religion to be untrue? And whence comes this strange idea that "religion" would tell the child that evil impulses come from the devil? Here once more is the recurrent lay-expert's fallacy of treating as universal and authoritative the theological opinions voiced by the minister's housemaid.

Is it not a cardinal principle of religion that God requireth truth in the inward parts, hating and abhorring a lying tongue? Truly, there is no hypocrisy so nauseating as the hypocrisy of the irreligious! See what is here implied. This is the prevalent attitude of the unbelieving world: it is worried about the consequences of religious unbelief *in others*. It wants the other fellow to behave as though decency, honour, trust, and fidelity were admitted social duties, while *we* enjoy the pleasures of irresponsible freedom. Why will not the children behave as properly brought-up Christians, with due respect for property, for their elders, for God, so that we, the adults and parents, can defy morality and God in comfort? Why will not the Communist bloc renounce atheism, violence, mendacity, and live as Christians, so that the Western world can pursue its divorces, its homosexuality, its gambling mania, its power-politics and worship of affluence, in uninterrupted peace? Why cannot the other fellow do the Christian thing, while I despise his scruples and scorn his faith?

Here is the old self-delusion that one can have the benefits of religion without its discipline, the order of society which only godliness produces without the individual submission to God's will which godliness demands. A child can see through it, not to mention a delinquent. And so can God.

46 "Suddenly . . . . "

THE suddenness of God is an idea somewhat out of fashion in these days. It has become obscured by our modern fondness for the complicated explanation of events; by our resolute faith in the slow, enduring processes by which great results are patiently prepared; by our shrewd investment in mills that grind with infinite gradualness, grain by grain, a final harvest of immeasurable good.

In frustrating years, when there is turmoil of conflicting trends against a background of fear, it is natural for courageous hearts to nourish thoughts of One keeping watch above His own, silently but surely moving forward to His goal. When the kingdom tarries, our minds cling tenaciously to faith's deeper insights, and we speak often of the steady onward pressure of invisible divine forces, moving irresistibly towards that far-off divine event on which our hopes are set.

There is nothing wrong, of course, with this patience of the saints. It is happily true that we look not at the things which are seen and that faith has always tomorrow. Yet continual emphasis upon the future can disguise evasion of the urgent personal issues involved in the present, the immediate demand for right reaction at this moment, in these present circumstances, to God's call in our existing situation. Insistence that great spiritual purposes must always mature slowly, that permanent results take time, may only rationalise a deep reluctance to act now, and energetically. What seems to be philosophic far-sightedness turns out to be mere procrastination!

Sooner or later the most patient divine preparation must land us on the threshold of fulfilment; the invisible spiritual processes must come to the point. Then God acts suddenly, not, of course, precipitately, but urgently, immediately, presenting an account upon which deferred payments will not do. Then men and nations face the moment to decide. The "inevitability of gradualness" may become as dangerous a cant phrase as "existential crisis"; the complete truth is, surely, that God prepares slowly to face us suddenly.

At any rate, "suddenly . . . the heavenly host" is a phrase to be kept beside the "Saviour promised long". Afterwards, the agelong preparations can be discerned, and the fullness of the times can be analysed and explained; but to the shepherds the revelation came with startling unexpectedness. Suddenly the opened heavens, the singing angels, the glorious light, the earth-changing news!

This is not exceptional. Unheralded crises are frequently the turning-points of Christian experience. Paul rides towards Damascus, intent upon his plans for the defence of Jewry against heretics, perhaps also absorbed with his inner discontents. "And suddenly there shined round about him a light from heaven." However long and deeply the shares of the Spirit had ploughed his soul, the crisis was momentary, the surrender instantaneous, the compact resolved and sealed before his companions could find their tongues.

Psychology's obsession with the subconscious mind has blunted, for some of us, the immediacy of the Bible's invitations, the urgency of the Bible's warnings, and by the same token has veiled in doubts the miracle of sudden conversion. However gently God prepares us, He finally confronts us with some conscious demand for decision and faith. The crucial moment may arrive quite suddenly, on our Damascus road — "today, if ye will hear his voice . . .".

Very often the great events of life are upon us without warning. Under the olive trees, "while Jesus yet spake, lo, Judas . . ." and tragedy. Paul and Silas lay in Philippi's town gaol, and "suddenly . . . a great earthquake" and deliverance. Two from Emmaus told what things were done in the way, and "as they thus spake, Jesus himself stood in the midst" and all was suddenly different. God need not aways knock when He visits His own.

The disciples wait, with one accord, in one place, preoccupied with memory and prayer, and doubtless with perplexed uncertainty as to what should happen next, "and suddenly . . . a rushing, mighty wind". It is not for us to know the times or seasons of spiritual renewal, of the "strangely warming" miracle that stirs a generation to seek its God again with contrite heart. But we can work in the confidence that new things are around the next corner. In a day of small things, the only adequate faith is that which expects great things from God, expects them *all the time.*

The suddenness of divine action, that is plainly a part of the truth concerning the first Advent of Christ, is almost the whole truth of the second. Always it is the unexpectedness of the end which Jesus emphasises: "Ye know not what hour your Lord doth come. . . . If the goodman of the house had known in what watch the thief would come, he would not have suffered his house to be broken into. . . . At midnight, behold a cry, The bridegroom . . . ." Master of the house, burglar, bridegroom — each arrives unheralded. "Watch ye therefore, lest coming *suddenly*, he find you sleeping."

Vigilance, wakefulness, expectancy, the tiptoe anticipation of some divine surprise, constitute the Advent virtues. Faith remembers that God retains the initiative; that the future is always different; that now is the accepted time; and today — whatever yesterday was like — today is the day of salvation.

47 Unto Him That Hath

IT is a teasing saying, in any of its forms: "Unto every one that hath shall be given, and he shall have abundance: but from him that hath not shall be taken away even that which he hath." It seems unfair. We quote it in envious cynicism when someone already wealthy inherits a fortune; we mutter it ruefully when someone already down is harder hit. Yet nothing could be farther from the spirit of Jesus than injustice and cynicism. What *could* He have meant?

For a start, the words convey neither warning nor promise. This is a statement of fact. Christ observes that this is the general experience of men; this is what happens, and will happen; this is the way of things, and always will be. And we know He is right.

That being clear, we begin to suspect that the words are a proverb, a shrewd summary of common experience current in the talk of the time. There is no doubt that Jesus did quote such proverbial, half-humorous sayings — "Sufficient to each day is its own load of evil"; and the sayings about swallowing a camel, the eye of a needle — just as any modern preacher might say, "A stitch in time . . ." or (on rare occasions!), "Silence is golden."

That would explain why the words are used on several occasions, about various things. The whole point of a proverb is that it summarises a truth so general, so obvious, that it applies to innumerable situations and illumines innumerable questions.

Five times the words appear in the Gospels, in slightly varying phrase, and we can discern at least three distinct applications of their truth.

Both Mark and Luke attach the saying to the Parable of the Sower, and surround it with warnings that make its meaning and truth abundantly clear. The seed that lies on the hard surface of the pathway yields no increase; only that which the earth truly "hath", by receiving it deep in the furrow and nourishing its life and growth, will bear fruit in the after days. So take heed, says Jesus, *how* you hear: "unto you that hear shall more be given".

Luke adds to these thoughts the image of the lamp set on its standard, or hidden under a vessel: light hidden is lost — "is taken away"; light shared is increased. To him who so listens, and hears, who retains and responds and reveals, more can be given; and that which he has increases of itself in value and power and meaning in his mind. But from him who but half attends, who hears with listless heart and unresponding conscience, even that glimpse of truth which nearly came will be taken away. There is no escape from this law. In the whole realm of knowledge we advance only by assimilation, by truly comprehending what we already think we know, and so moving forward to new truth. But when, as with Christian truth, the knowledge concerned is essentially practical, a way of living as well as a way of thinking, then this law holds with still greater rigour. Only he that hath . . . is ready to learn more.

Both Matthew and Luke attach this same saying to their versions of the parable of service — the "Talents" and the "Pounds". Here it is not knowledge but gifts and opportunities that are in question, and the means whereby a man may "graduate" from the lesser responsibility to the greater, from the smaller capacity to the "ten-talent" class. The meaning is scarcely in question: only those who truly possess what lies already to hand can be, or should be, entrusted with more.

It could not be otherwise. To those who show readiness, give diligence, seize opportunities, accept responsibility, the most desired of all rewards will be more challenge and wider opportunity and heavier responsibility! But from those upon whom these things are wasted, they must be taken away before they slip through their fingers. Usefulness, responsibility, influence, power, and opportunity are not things that can be given a man: they must be prepared for; in the last resort they must be deserved, by faithfulness in that which is least.

Too often we sit waiting for the great call to come, dreaming meanwhile of the wonderful things we shall do when the door opens for us and the opportunities beckon. But the call remains silent, the door shut, the opportunity never comes —

just because we sat and dreamed. The things we longed for cannot be bestowed — unto him that hath, they come!

Matthew, too, attaches the saying to the Parable of the Sower, but in quite his own way. First he recalls another word of Jesus, about the "mysteries of the kingdom" and those to whom it is given to know them. Immediately afterwards he adds strange words about some who see without perceiving and hear without understanding, because their hearts are grown gross, their ears dull, their eyes are closed, lest they turn to God. In this setting of thought he places the words that puzzle us: "Unto him that hath . . .".

Plainly, the meaning is very near to that of Mark and Luke concerning knowledge; but Matthew, it seems, is thinking of deeper experience, of the relation of the soul to God, of the continuing exploration of all the "mystery" of living under God's gracious rule.

Here once again is a realm of experience where the prizes cannot be *given*. We learn faith by trusting, by taking risks for God, by obeying in spite of the consequences, and leaving the outcome with Him. We learn more of His will by doing what already we know He would have us do, by pondering with teachable spirit the things that already He has said to our hearts. We learn prayer by praying — there just *can* be no other way. We experience His love, the joy of His presence, the peace of His care for our hearts by simply resting in the fact that He is our God, our Father, and our Friend.

Such is the necessary rule of all spiritual progress: the law of advancing insight, the law of increasing usefulness, the law of deepening experience. To appreciate and use is to attain still more; to neglect and despise is to forfeit what you have. "Unto him that hath . . . *and from him that hath not . . . .*"

48 God Is Greater

TWICE within a few verses John, in his epistle, declares that "God is greater . . .". There is nothing remarkable in the reiteration itself: the Bible constantly insists that all our imagination, our words, our imagery and our worship cannot express the greatness of God or worthily represent His matchless glory. What does make us pause upon John's repetition is the unusual application he makes of the truth he asserts.

The second time, he is addressing the all-too-familiar mood of spiritual discouragement, that special form of discouragement that arises from self-depreciation. His readers have seen once trusted leaders and teachers desert the apostolic fellowship and go out to found communities of their own supporters. These men have prospered; their new version of the gospel has proved popular; crowds flock to their meetings. On the other hand, the apostolic groups find the work hard, their numbers dwindling, and the world inattentive.

John's answer is brusque: the world welcomes its own! They are of the world and they speak the things of the world. What then? Greater is He that is in you than He that is in the world!

The self-depreciating mood that plays up our own failure or incapacity, as an excuse for giving in, is an insidious temptation for the people of God: it *sounds* so like humility! Elijah deplores that he only is left and doomed; Gideon pleads that he is least in his father's house; Moses argues that he is not eloquent — and does it eloquently. Jeremiah apparently shirked his call on the plea that he was too young. The man with one talent makes the smallness of his opportunity the excuse for doing nothing at all.

The strong and sound reply to this undermining mood is not flattery but faith. It does not deceive us. It does not tell us that we are much more important than we suppose, invaluable indeed, almost irreplaceable! Instead, it reminds us that God who is in us is greater than all that is against us. So very often when we estimate our chances of success and add up the opposing factors in any situation that depresses us, we leave out God — the hardest Fact of all, the Immeasurable Statistic.

Even more often when we are estimating ourselves, and assessing what we can or cannot do in the work of the kingdom, we leave out God, and what He could make of us, what He wants to make of us, if we will but try.

The first time John mentions the greatness of God he is addressing the much rarer mood of spiritual discouragement that arises from self-accusation. Rare, indeed, except among the most sensitive souls, the tenderest consciences! Yet if proud hearts need humbling, if those who think they stand should take heed lest they fall, no less certain is it that sometimes very humble hearts need to be lifted to the full assurance of faith, and earnest and anxious piety established in Christian confidence.

Self-accusation, too, can unfit us for divine opportunity and unnerve us in the face of spiritual opportunity. The centurion's "I am not worthy", and even more Peter's "Depart from me, for I am a sinful man", might well have cost the speakers dearly had not Christ been greater than their own hearts. Isaiah's "Woe is me . . . a man of unclean lips" is not allowed to cancel his call to be a prophet; nor is Israel's "The Lord has cast us off" accepted as excuse for not rising up and returning to the city of their fathers. "With the Lord there is mercy, and with him is plenteous redemption." "How much kinder God is to us," remarks Anthony Trollope, "than we are willing to be to ourselves!"

So Paul argues: "Who shall condemn, when God justifies?" There is no condemnation to them that are in Christ. Even if we be faithless, He abideth faithful: the Lord *knoweth* them that are His. That last thought is John's too: "God is greater than your heart, and knoweth all things." The only fitting illustration is hackneyed, but still bears repeating. Jesus confronts Peter on the lake side after Easter, and makes him retrace his threefold denial by a threefold confession of love. The implications tear Peter's heart, until the third time he can only protest brokenly, remembering the denial and the swearing, but remembering also the remorse and the self-despising and the weeping bitterly — "Lord, thou knowest all things, thou knowest that I love thee!"

Indeed He does, and knowing all, forgives us oftentimes the things we may be too proud to forgive ourselves.

49   The Spiritual World

PERHAPS the deepest difference between the Bible's characters and ourselves lies in their sharp awareness of the spiritual world. Many of them had hard lives, and felt the same pervading insecurity that afflicts us. They knew the world passeth away, but they were far surer than we are that another, eternal world was all about them. They knew they had only to open their eyes to see the cavalry of the Lord of Hosts — horses and chariots of fire — surrounding them on all sides. We are not so certain. It rarely *feels* like it!

It was not only Elisha and his servant at Dothan. From beginning to end the Bible is full of people to whom God and the spiritual world were everyday assumptions. Abraham journeys from place to place at the direction of a divine voice; he marks the stages of his pilgrimage with altars where we would put gasoline stations. Moses talks familiarly with God on Sinai; Isaiah attends a royal funeral and sees a greater King; Joshua the soldier meets the Captain of the Lord's army, with a drawn sword in His hand; Gideon argues with angels; Elijah argues with God on Horeb; Hezekiah reads the evening's mail to God; Nehemiah rebuilds the walls of Jerusalem with mingled pride and prayer.

Peter watches in dismay as fish are caught with divine skill; Paul is smitten blind by excess of light, and lives thereafter in the explosion of divine power; the seer on Patmos hears in the roar of the sea the divine Voice like the sound of many waters, and pens a masterpiece of insight and courage. This is the Bible way of life: heaven lies about man in the world's infancy. Moses endured as seeing Him who is invisible, Paul looked upon things not seen but eternal, and John could never forget he had leaned on the breast of God. To such men the spiritual world was the most real — or at any rate the most lasting, and meaningful, and important. They took the existence of God for granted. The laws and warnings and rewards of the spiritual realm were the axioms of their lives.

But we have to argue ourselves into their assumptions. We must school ourselves to know and feel what they intuitively experienced. Nothing could be more important for modern folk, for our behaviour, our faith, our inspiration and resources and hope, than to attain to the same first-hand certainty, the same instinctive awareness, of the presence of God about us, and the reality of the world beyond the earth.

One secret, surely, is to think more deeply. We must really ponder the world that is about us to see the "miracles" of mind and spirit that are already there. Memory vaguely recalls the assertion that New York's Empire State Building is "a gigantic spiritual fact". Few things might seem more solid, material, or obvious! Yet it is an intellectual miracle throughout: a perfectly balanced equation of forces, weight balancing strength, the pull of gravity against the uncrushability of stone, the thrust of storm against the tensile strength of steel and the moment of inertia. It is a mighty thought, a design in stone and steel that — if you take away the mere mathematics — would crumble in ruins.

We so often, and so foolishly, suppose we have explained the event when we have discovered the method, explained the fact when we have laid bare its parts. We analyse the flower into carbon, magnesium, oxygen, chlorophyll or whatever, and think these made the flower! We demonstrate the social forces behind the triumph of Christianity in the Roman world and think we have "explained" the Christian martyrdoms! We dissect the muscle-movements of a kiss and suppose we know what young love is! Much of our unbelief stems from our inability to think twice, our want of insight, our absorption with the obvious to the exclusion of the essentially mysterious beneath the surface of our definitions. The spiritual world of reason, purpose, power, life and love is all about us, interpenetrating all we see and touch and use.

> O world invisible, we view thee,
> O world intangible, we touch thee,
> O world unknowable, we know thee,
> Inapprehensible, we clutch thee!
>
> Does the fish soar to find the ocean,
> The eagle plunge to find the air. . . .

The angels keep their ancient places;
Turn but a stone, and start a wing!
'Tis ye, 'tis your estranged faces
That miss the many-splendoured thing.

Awareness of the spiritual world requires purity as well as perceptiveness. "Badness keeps one from the realisation of God," says Rose Macaulay, adding a poignant comment about long years of wrongdoing building a kind of blank — or nearly blank — wall between oneself and God. Without a clear or cleansed conscience, the sense of God and a vivid awareness of spiritual realities are beyond our reach. Sensuality, revengefulness, cruelty, deceit, selfishness, even slothfulness, can numb the soul's antennae and blur the vision of the heart. As centuries ago a Hebrew poet confessed, "If I had cherished iniquity in my heart, the Lord would not have listened" — evidently the transcript of some sad experience.

Without holiness, no man shall see the Lord. Did not Jesus Himself declare that the blessedness of the pure in heart lies in just this, that *they* see God?

Although want of perceptiveness, or want of purity, is the trouble with most of us, something must be added about practice. The Christian cannot live upon his feelings, but he ought not to live without them, without the felt sense of divine blessing coming upon him from time to time. When uplifting worship, answered prayer, clear divine guidance, rewarding communion, satisfying service of Christ's cause, the upsurging joy of knowing Him, become just the distant memories of early Christian life, then something is seriously wrong. Nor should such experiences of God's approach be just the rare high days upon the mountaintop, occurring once or twice a year. God does not intend it so, and when it happens with us it is not His fault. There is no reason at all why we should live on a sub-Christian level, with all the promises of God within our hands and Christ beside us.

Perhaps, like the young man at Dothan, we, too, need opened eyes. We would not be the first disciples to walk with Jesus on a weary road with eyes holden that we do not know Him.

50 Barren Harvests

IN the somewhat sophisticated company gathered at a dinner in Paris, an American ambassador, Benjamin Franklin, is said to have recited an exquisite, ancient poem which was greeted with delighted enthusiasm — until its source was revealed. For, so the story runs, it was the closing passage of the book of Habakkuk:

> For though the fig tree shall not blossom
> Neither shall fruit be in the vines;
> The labour of the olive shall fail,
> And the fields shall yield no meat;
> The flock shall be cut off from the fold,
> And there shall be no herd in the stalls:
> Yet I will rejoice in the Lord,
> I will joy in the God of my salvation.
> Jehovah, the Lord, is my strength,
> He maketh my feet like the feet of the hinds —
> He will make me to walk on high places!

As an expression of religious faith and certainty, of joyous, radiant trust in the providence of God, this is hardly to be paralleled in the whole Bible.

Perhaps the poetic form and Oriental setting blur something of the prophet's meaning for prosaic Western minds. Remember that figs and vines and olives and crops provided work and wealth for the Israelite, and translate:

> Though the factories stand idle and the mines are deserted; though gardens and fields are barren and the shops are empty; though business fails, work ceases and health and home are taken from us — yet will we rejoice in the Lord: though my world totter around me and my security perish overnight, yet will I joy in the God of my salvation."

Something like this reflects Habakkuk's spirit and reveals his rightful place as the Bible's finest spokesman of one level of devotion.

There is another kind of religion, even in the Bible. "*If* God will be with me, and keep me in this way that I go, and will give me bread to eat and raiment to put on, so that I come again to my father's house in peace, *then* shall the Lord be my God." So Jacob, at Bethel. Such was the attitude of Job's friends, seeing in his calamities a certain proof that Job was not a godly man — for what was godliness for, but to insure against adversity? Such was the attitude of the Galilean crowd that followed Jesus for the loaves and fishes. It reaches its terrible climax in the bitter disappointment of worldly hopes that prompted Judas' treachery.

A prayer is ascribed, perhaps in satire, to an English business-man of the eighteenth century, in the following terms: "O Lord, Thou knowest that I have nine houses in the city of London, and that I have lately purchased an estate in Essex: I beseech Thee to preserve the two counties of Middlesex and Essex from fires and earthquakes, and for the rest do what Thou wilt." That reduces Jacob-religion to absurdity — the love of God for what we can get out of Him, and a loyalty to Him that is conditional upon His coming up to our expectations! To such a faith adversity constitutes a fatal problem; at the first breath of trouble such religion dissolves in disillusionment.

Far different is the faith of our poet-prophet; or of the Psalmist who in adversity will cling to God though pouring out complaints; or of Job who will cling to God with uncomplaining doggedness — "Though he slay me, yet will I trust him"; or of Paul, who will cling to God, believing that all things work together for good. Even Paul does not rise higher than Habakkuk, who in adversity will cling to God radiantly, joyfully, though he has no explanation to lean upon and none to offer.

In E. Tegla Davies' fine short story, a poor Welsh farmer, Samuel Jones, found himself out of tune with the harvest thanksgivings of his wealthier neighbours. They could decorate the little chapel with a proud display of fruit and vegetables that told of highly successful husbandry; he had only meagre crops wrested from sun-starved, weed-choked land that repaid ill his harder toil. One year the bitter contrast was too sharp; he resolved not to attend, to let the harvest celebration and the anthems and the thanksgiving prayer meeting do without him. A long night's walk alone, half in self-pity, half in prayer, brought new insight. Early on harvest morning he went to the chapel, and greatly daring, removed the fruit and flowers, the luscious vegetables and ripe corn of his neighbours' gifts, and replaced them with his own nettles and weeds, his docks and brambles.

At service time the congregation was dumb, bewildered, angry. How could men see God's goodness in thistles and brambles and gorse, or sing thanksgiving in the face of disappointment, and poverty, and barren fields? Samuel Jones for once took the pulpit, and with the sympathy of all, with his new insight into the meaning of faith shining in his eyes, read with his soul in every word:

> *Though the fig tree shall not blossom,*
> *Neither shall fruit be in the vines,*
> *The labour of the olive shall fail . . .*
> *Yet will I rejoice in the Lord,*
> *I will joy in the God of my salvation!*

And then he led the congregation in a prayer of trust and praise and joy that is remembered by all who heard.

That is true worship: unseeking, unconditioned faith that with Thomas à Kempis "regardeth not the gift of the lover but the love of the giver". Letting God do what He chooses about the vines and figs and stalls, confident that the heavenly Father knows we have need of these things, and in whatsoever state we are, therein to be content: such is the secret not only of worship, and of peace, but of a constant joy in God that treads sure-footed on high places as hinds in the springtime and finds its strength not in gifts and providences and answered prayer, but in God Himself.

51 Companions of Truth

THE famous aphorism about preaching being truth through personality usually serves to focus attention upon the individual behind the sermon, upon the very human vessels in which the treasure of the gospel is offered to men, upon the limitations of knowledge, the tricks and mannerisms of thought and gesture through which the truth must filter. It is a fine definition, though its application is sometimes one-sided.

It is odd that even in our Reformed tradition, amongst those who habitually preach or suffer sermons, the questions commonly asked about a preacher concern his art — his power to interest, his wit, imagination, charm — rather than his message. It is odd, because at heart we all know that the substance is more vital than the technique, and that the mighty weapon of pulpit oratory is reduced to impotence if behind the poetry and anecdote and phrase-making there is no incisive edge of truth. It is truth, not personality, that upbuilds the Church. Neither the preaching nor the hearing of sermons is well accomplished until there rises in the soul the simple comment: "That's very true!"

Yet to be a purveyor of truth in Vanity Fair is no sinecure. We peddle unpopular wares. The lament of the prophet befits our time also — that truth is fallen in the street, and few will pause to help her to her feet. We speak to a generation with suspicious ears, trained to subtract from all it hears the things it assumes are due to the hidden motives of the speaker. Thinking people, from Pilate to the Positivists, dismiss the very possibility of truth as an objective test of opinion. Unthinking people reach the same conclusion by assuming outright that what they believe must necessarily be the truth. The great number whose job it is to persuade the unthinking — politicians, advertisers, and the like — give up all pretence of truth and turn to techniques of persuasion which appeal to suggestion, emotion, pride, avarice, or sex, and which have no relation to reason or to fact at all. The purveyor of truth finds his stall unattended, his wares in surplus supply, his methods of salesmanship sadly outmoded.

It is not alone in the atmosphere of our time that truth suffers. Sometimes in church she walks shyly, like a poor relation. We are anxious that she keep to the narrow path of orthodoxy, and are a little scandalised by her flirtatious fondness for the company of freedom. We forget that it was the Master who first coupled these together; and while we like the thought that truth shall make men free, the converse troubles us — that only freedom will keep you true.

So we tend to fetter the enquiring mind, to bar the irreverent question, to proscribe the "unsound" books, to impose a ready-made formula upon the exploring spirit. It all betrays sad lack of faith in truth's power to defend herself. It also betrays a sad failure to learn from experience.

The finest statement of faith, erected into a compulsory pattern of thought, an intellectual procrustean bed, a wicket gate through which all must pass who wish to get on, becomes *inevitably* a shibboleth, a sham, a mere intellectual pose. Where freedom to enquire is denied — whether by the state, by priestcraft, or by bigotry — there truth withers. Only the freedom to follow the Spirit of truth wherever He leads can keep faith true.

We also have the idea that truth rests with the majority. Surely, what the many think cannot be wrong! Majorities are the last court of appeal. If an idea is steadily gaining ground with an increasing number of people, then it must be (in some curious way) in process of becoming true! "Eighty percent of those questioned replied . . . which proves . . . ." "Crowds will flock where the old gospel truth is faithfully preached. . . . Look at A......'s church, look at B......'s campaign!" (Don't look, though, at St. Peter's Rome: that's another story!)

Numbers are evidence of authority. The popularity of an idea proves its inherent power — and so its veracity. That is why we must find unity: the world will listen to the mass expression of Christian opinion, uttered by so many millions speaking in unison. It is all very persuasive; but it needs great care. A proposition is not necessarily true just because many folk believe it. An idea is not necessarily valid because it promotes

143

unity of mind. Truth cannot be decided by a show of hands. All history witnesses that isolated spirits sometimes see most deeply, that the pioneers plod alone, and are too often stoned by the multitude — or crucified. Truth is so often a voice crying in the wilderness, with only the birds to hear. Truth's dour companion, loneliness, is ill-favoured and unpopular.

Her third companion is integrity. Truth is an austere mistress, demanding to be obeyed as well as defended, asking in her champions transparency and courage, forthrightness of character and plainness of speech. Unfortunately, we have to entice people to listen to us, we are fearful of giving offence, urgently concerned to keep the peace. The guarded opinion, the too effusive praise, the evasive reply seem simple prudence — though truth is hurt. What fresh air might circulate through church corridors if a Quaker accuracy of speech became the fashion!

A great New Testament theme confronts us here. According to John, truth is first believed, as news; then submitted to, as discipline; and then it dwells in us, as the source of life. Freedom, loneliness, integrity are exacting conditions; yet in acceptance of the truth lies our salvation, in service of the truth lies all authority and power, in the unshaken endurance and sure victory of truth lies all our hope and confidence.

52 The Way Ahead

THE sin of the golden calf had brought to a standstill Israel's pilgrimage towards Canaan. The Tables of the Covenant were broken, the future imperilled. It looked almost as though God had revoked His promise to His people, as though the glorious vision of redemption would fade and fail. But Moses intercedes. The tables are renewed, the sin is forgiven, the tents are struck, and the journey restarts. It is a new beginning, marked with new mercy. Setting forward again with chastened heart Moses prays: Show me now Thy way.

Therein the patriarch speaks for all of us, voicing the cry of the godly in every generation for a lamp for their feet. Modern man may be incredibly skilful in threading a path across the trackless skies, but he is not noticeably more successful than his fathers in finding the way to wholeness and happiness, security and peace. We, too, have learned that there is a way that seemeth right unto a man, but the end thereof is the way of death.

Amid the clamour of conflicting voices man is as truly lost as ever he was, at sea in a universe too big for him, confused by problems too complicated for him, helpless before forces too strong for him, persuading himself that he is striving all the while towards a goal he no longer believes in. What else should he plead, but *Show me now Thy way?*

The growing child, imposed upon by all the tensions and contradictions of our discordant society — how complicated life has become for him! The tempted youth, beset by a hundred allurements to evil, justifying excuses, and undermining arguments — how shall a young man keep clean his way? The responsible parent, teacher, leader, man of affairs, in a society that lacks cohesion, moral purpose, and direction — how shall he keep his way clear, his vision unclouded, amid the perplexities and dogmatisms of the day? The earnest Christian, struggling to apply an ancient faith to unprecedented situations, torn by conflicting loyalties, faced constantly by the heart-searching necessity of distinguishing the permanent, timeless truth from its changing, temporary forms — how often he prays, "Teach us thy way, O Lord, and lead us in a plain path."

The answer which Moses received exceeded all his asking. "My presence shall go with thee." He asked instruction and was given companionship. He sought a signpost and was given a Guide. So God always answers. The journey through the wilderness cannot be foreseen or mapped out with waymarks; no codes and rules of past ages suffice for new times and fresh problems. The path of the just is not to be found merely in ancient laws and buried wisdom: it is learned by walking with God.

145

Hand in hand, step by step, we move through life with God, listening for His voice through every avenue by which He speaks to men, keeping the conscience alert, the heart obedient, the spirit humble. The way cannot simply be pointed out to us or described in the language of another's life-experience. God Himself is the answer to our cry because He *is* the Way.

That is the central picture of the twenty-third Psalm: "the Lord is my Guide — He leads me by right paths for the sake of His own reputation; though I walk through a valley as dark as death, I will not fear, for Thy defending club and upholding staff afford me courage!"

That, too, is the promise of Jesus: "He that followeth me shall not walk in darkness, but shall have the light of life." "My presence shall go with thee." That is better than light and safer than a known way.

Yet Moses asked for more: "Show me thy glory." The people are stubborn, the way is long and hard, disappointments press upon him, the memory of failure burdens his heart. He longs to lift his soul above the task, the confusion, the demands, and to see God's glory. Given that vision, the task becomes inspiring, the confusion resolves, the demands seem a compliment; but without it, to see God's way stretch challengingly ahead may daunt the bravest.

This prayer, too, was answered. Israel, it is recorded, "saw God's glory" at four significant places: at Sinai, where her obedience was renewed; at the giving of the manna, where her faith was justified; at the gushing of water from the rock, where her unbelief was shamed; at the erection of the Tabernacle, where her altar fires were kindled. We, too, shall see His glory.

But suggestive as all this is, the full answer to the prayer again excelled the asking. Moses prayed to see God's *glory*: he was promised the vision of God's *goodness* — "I will make all my goodness to pass before thee." That, surely, is the deepest truth in all God's revelation. *The glory of God is His goodness* — His loving-kindness, His gentleness, His never-tiring patience, and His never-slumbering pity. This we shall see as we go forward bravely in His way: the glory that is goodness, and the everlasting splendour that is full of grace and truth.

146